science for a changing world

Prepared in cooperation with the U.S. Army Corps of Engineers

Channel Change and Bed-Material Transport in the Lower Chetco River, Oregon

By J. Rose Wallick, Scott W. Anderson, Charles Cannon, and Jim E. O'Connor

Open-File Report 2009–1163

U.S. Department of the Interior
U.S. Geological Survey

U.S. Department of the Interior
KEN SALAZAR, Secretary

U.S. Geological Survey
Suzette M. Kimball, Acting Director

U.S. Geological Survey, Reston, Virginia: 2009

For product and ordering information:
World Wide Web: http://www.usgs.gov/pubprod
Telephone: 1-888-ASK-USGS

For more information on the USGS—the Federal source for science about the Earth,
its natural and living resources, natural hazards, and the environment:
World Wide Web: http://www.usgs.gov
Telephone: 1-888-ASK-USGS

Suggested citation:
Wallick, J.R., Anderson, S.W., Cannon, Charles, and O'Connor, J.E., 2009,
Channel change and bed-material transport in the lower Chetco River, Oregon:
U.S. Geological Survey Open-File Report 2009–1163, 83 p.

Contents

Figures

Tables

Conversion Factors

Multiply	By	To obtain
Length		
centimeter (cm)	0.3937	Inch (in.)
millimeter (mm)	0.03937	inch (in.)
meter (m)	3.281	foot (ft)
kilometer (km)	0.6214	mile (mi)
Area		
square meter (m^2)	10.76	square foot (ft^2)
square kilometer (km^2)	0.3861	square mile (mi^2)
Volume		
cubic meter (m^3)	0.0008107	acre-foot (acre-ft)
cubic meter (m^3)	35.31	cubic foot (ft^3)
cubic meter (m^3)	1.308	cubic yard (yd^3)
liter (L)	0.03531	cubic foot (ft^3)
Flow rate		
cubic meter per second (m^3/s)	35.31	cubic foot per second (ft^3/s)
cubic meter per year (m^3/yr)	1.308	cubic yard per year (yd^3/yr)
meter per second (m/s)	3.281	foot per second (ft/s)
meter per year (m/yr)	3.281	foot per year (ft/yr)
millimeter per year (mm/yr)	0.0397	inch per year (in/yr)
kilogram per meter per second	4.486	pound avoirdupois per foot per second (lb/ft/s)
Mass		
kilogram (kg)	2.205	pound avoirdupois (lb)

Datums

Vertical coordinate information is referenced to the North American Vertical Datum of 1988 (NAVD 88). Horizontal coordinate information is referenced to the North American Datum of 1983 (NAD 83). Elevation, as used in this report, refers to distance above the vertical datum.

Abbreviations and Acronyms

BAGS	Bedload Assessment in Gravel-bedded Streams
BLM	Bureau of Land Management
GPS	global positioning system
HEC-RAS	Hydrologic Engineering Center's River Analysis System
MLLW	mean lower low water
RMSE	root mean square error
RTK	real-time kinematic
USFS	U.S. Forest Service
USGS	U.S. Geological Survey

Channel Change and Bed-Material Transport in the Lower Chetco River, Oregon

By J. Rose Wallick, Scott W. Anderson, Charles Cannon, and Jim E. O'Connor

Abstract

The lower Chetco River is a wandering gravel-bed river flanked by abundant and large gravel bars formed of coarse bed-material sediment. The large gravel bars have been a source of commercial aggregate since the early twentieth century for which ongoing permitting and aquatic habitat concerns have motivated this assessment of historical channel change and sediment transport rates. Analysis of historical channel change and bed-material transport rates for the lower 18 kilometers show that the upper reaches of the study area are primarily transport zones, with bar positions fixed by valley geometry and active bars mainly providing transient storage of bed material. Downstream reaches, especially near the confluence of the North Fork Chetco River, have been zones of active sedimentation and channel migration.

Multiple analyses, supported by direct measurements of bedload during winter 2008–09, indicate that since 1970 the mean annual flux of bed material into the study reach has been about 40,000–100,000 cubic meters per year. Downstream tributary input of bed-material sediment, probably averaging 5–30 percent of the influx coming into the study reach from upstream, is approximately balanced by bed-material attrition by abrasion. Probably very little bed material leaves the lower river under natural conditions, with most of the net influx historically accumulating in wider and more dynamic reaches, especially near the North Fork Chetco River confluence, 8 kilometers upstream from the Pacific Ocean.

The year-to-year flux, however, varies tremendously. Some years probably have less than 3,000 cubic meters of bed-material entering the study area; by contrast, some high-flow years, such as 1982 and 1997, likely have more than 150,000 cubic meters entering the reach. For comparison, the estimated annual volume of gravel extracted from the lower Chetco River for commercial aggregate during 2000–2008 has ranged from 32,000 to 90,000 cubic meters and averaged about 59,000 cubic meters per year. Mined volumes probably exceeded 140,000 cubic meters per year for several years in the late 1970s.

Repeat surveys and map analyses indicate a reduction in bar area and sinuosity between 1939 and 2008, chiefly in the period 1965–95. Repeat topographic and bathymetric surveys show channel incision for substantial portions of the study reach, with local areas of bed lowering by as much as 2 meters. A specific gage analysis at the upstream end of the study reach indicates that incision and narrowing followed aggradation culminating in the late 1970s. These observations are all consistent with a reduction of sediment supply relative to transport capacity since channel surveys in the late 1970s, probably owing to a combination of (1) bed-sediment removal and (2) transient river adjustments to large sediment volumes brought by floods such as those in 1964, and to a lesser extent, 1996.

Introduction

The Chetco River is a steep gravel-bed river in southwestern Oregon draining 914 square kilometers (km²) of the rugged Klamath Mountains before entering the Pacific Ocean 5 kilometers (km) north of the California–Oregon State line (fig. 1). Downstream of the confluence of the South Fork Chetco River at river kilometer (Rkm) 29, the Chetco River is flanked by varying widths and areas of gravel bars and floodplains. Downstream of Rkm 18, several of these gravel bars have been mined as a source of aggregate for the last century. Ongoing permitting actions have instigated questions of possible effects from such mining on physical channel conditions (for example, Kondolf, 1994, 1997), prompting the U.S. Army Corps of Engineers, in conjunction with regulatory agencies and stakeholder groups, to request from the U.S. Geological Survey (USGS) a measurement and analysis program to evaluate transport rates of bed material and to assess changes in channels and floodplains for the lower 18 km.

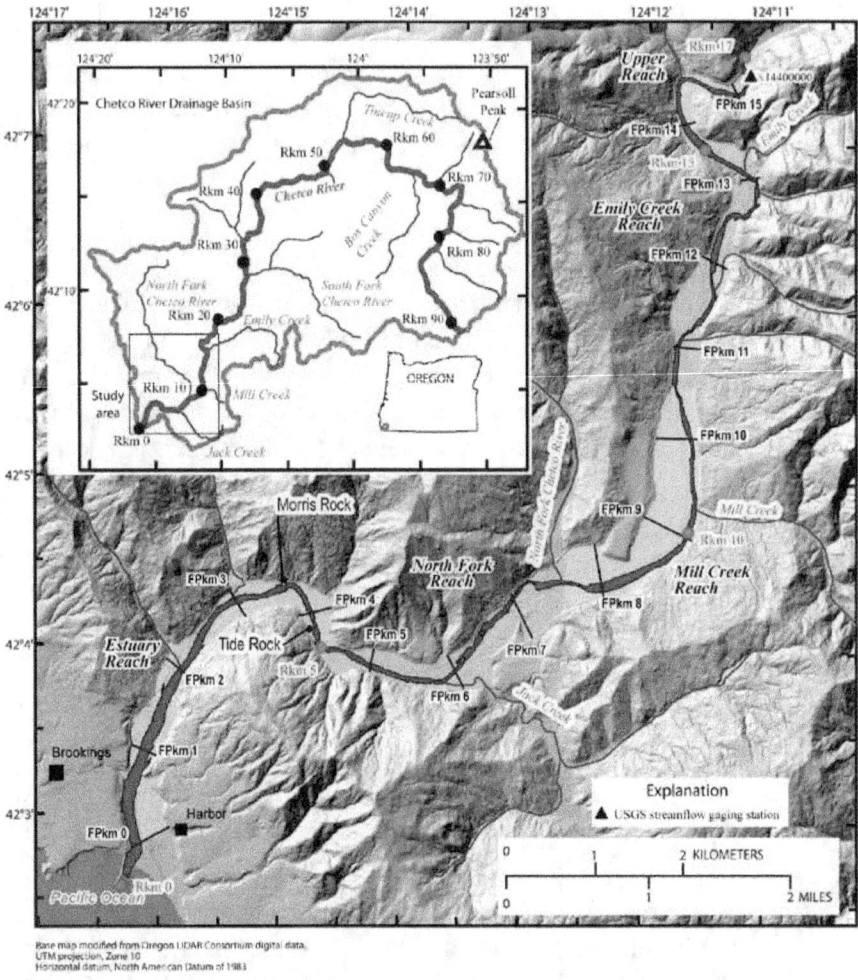

Figure 1. Map showing watershed and study area, Chetco River, Oregon. Morris Rock and Tide Rock are informal names for prominent local landmarks. Topography based on U.S. Geological Survey 10-m digital elevation data and 2008 LIDAR topography. Rkm, river kilometer; FPkm, floodplain kilometer.

Purpose and Scope

This report summarizes analyses of temporal trends in channel width and gravel bar area, and bed-material transport measurements and calculations, with the goal to estimate temporal and spatial trends in bedload transport, deposition, and erosion within the lowermost 18 km of the Chetco River, and further to assess historical changes to the channel and floodplain. These analyses were supported by systematic mapping of channels and floodplains from historical and current aerial photographs, sampling of bed-material size distributions, bedload transport measurements and hydraulic modeling. Additionally, the channel mapping in conjunction with new surveys allows for assessment of planform and vertical changes in channels, possibly attributable to changes in sediment balances and transport. The scope of the study follows from a process established in the State of Oregon to address permitting issues for inchannel gravel extraction.

Background

The Chetco River is like many western U.S. rivers for which issues of fish habitat, water quality, climate change, and changing land use have motivated new efforts to manage rivers and floodplains for multiple resources. Within Oregon, rivers potentially subject to inchannel gravel extraction undergo a two-phase process of review and assessment by an interagency team co-chaired by the U.S. Army Corps of Engineers and the Oregon Department of State Lands, and subdivided into an executive team of policy managers and a technical team of supporting resource experts. The first phase is a preliminary assessment of "vertical stability" based primarily on available information. If Phase I analysis shows no clear evidence of adverse channel or floodplain conditions, a Phase II analysis may be initiated to provide more information relevant to permitting decisions. For the Chetco River, this Phase I assessment was completed in May 2007 (Janine Castro, U.S. Fish and Wildlife Service, written commun., 2007). This assessment of maps and surveys concluded that although the lowermost 2 km of the river "appears to have deepened slightly over the past 20 years," there was no evidence of systematic channel incision for the balance of the lower 18 km of the Chetco River. These findings prompted the executive team to consider permitting of future instream gravel extraction upon completion of a more extensive Phase II analysis consisting of data acquisition and analysis aimed at:

1. Determining spatial and temporal rates of bed-material transport.

2. Assessing planform and vertical changes to the river channel.

In addition to these specific Phase II analysis components, the USGS was requested to provide broadscale maps of floodplain geomorphology and general vegetation along the floodplain flanking the lower 18 km of the river corridor. The lower 18 km forms a convenient analysis segment because the upstream end approximately corresponds to the USGS streamflow measurement station for the Chetco River 16.9 km upstream from the mouth and encompasses the extent of commercial gravel extraction. These findings and maps will be used by the regulatory agencies as supporting information for future permitting decisions for instream gravel extraction along the Chetco River.

Our approaches for assessing channel changes, as well as mapping current and historical channels and vegetation, followed established procedures of aerial photograph analysis, and channel and floodplain surveys. Our analysis period extends back to include aerial photographs and bathymetric surveys from 1939. Assessing sediment transport rates and budgets is more difficult (Reid and Dunne, 1996, 2003), particularly for bed material (Edwards and Glysson, 1999; Hicks and Gomez, 2003; Reid and Dunne, 2003). Because of the challenges in assessing bed-material transport rates, we have adopted several measurement, modeling, and analysis approaches to ensure the greatest likelihood of meaningful results and to provide qualitative assessment of their accuracy.

Units and Locations

All analyses and results are presented in metric units. Conversions to English units are provided in the report front matter. Locations along the channel alignment in summer 2008 are referenced to river kilometers (Rkm) measured from the Chetco River mouth along the channel centerline mapped from Light Detection and Ranging (LIDAR) topography acquired in 2008. Ambiguity because of channel shifting was avoided by referencing locations and analyses for the lowermost 18 km to a floodplain centerline (FPkm), measured from the river mouth along the centerline of the Holocene floodplain (fig. 1). In 2008, approximately 18 km of channel were within the 16-km-long length of floodplain composing the study reach. Prominent landmarks and locations include the Highway 101 bridge at FPkm 0.9 (Rkm 1.4), Tide Rock at FPkm 4.2 (Rkm 4.9), North Fork Chetco River confluence at FPkm 7.6 (Rkm 8.3), and the USGS streamflow measurement station (at Second Bridge) at FPkm 15.2 (Rkm 16.9).

The Chetco River

The Chetco River drains 914 km^2 of southwestern Oregon and empties into the Pacific Ocean 5 km north of the California-Oregon border (fig. 1). Major tributaries are Tincup Creek (Rkm 54), South Fork Chetco River (Rkm 29), and North Fork Chetco River (Rkm 8.3; FPkm 7.6). In 1988, the Chetco River between Rkm 16 and 88 was designated as "Wild and Scenic" as part of the National Wild and Scenic River program. The eastern half of the drainage basin is within the Kalmiopsis Wilderness Area, established in 1964. At its entrance to the Pacific, the river separates the coastal communities of Brookings and Harbor. The drainage basin is wholly contained within Curry County, Oregon.

Geography and Geology

The drainage basin is steep and rugged. The highest point is Pearsoll Peak at 1,554 m, and the lowest elevation is sea level at the river mouth. The average basin slope is 0.42 m/m as measured from 10-m resolution digital elevation data. Drainage density, as measured from the 1:24,000 National Hydrologic Data set is 1.4 km/km^2. The Chetco River itself is 88 km long, heading at an elevation of 540 m and descending to sea level at an average gradient of 0.006 m/m, but most elevation loss is in the upper half of the drainage basin, leaving the lowermost 38 km with a gradient of 0.0013.

The drainage basin is within the Klamath Mountains physiographic province, an amalgamation of several geologic terranes affixed to western North America during the late Mesozoic and early Tertiary in a progression of eastward dipping underthrusts. During accretion and subsequently, the rocks have been metamorphosed and intruded by igneous plutons, dikes, and sills, chiefly of Cretaceous and Tertiary age. The degree of metamorphism and igneous intrusive activity decreases westward, with most of the highly deformed metamorphic rock and intrusive igneous rocks forming the steeper and higher eastern part of the drainage basin, mainly upstream of Rkm 70. The western half of the basin is dominated by the Dothan Formation, which consists mainly of slightly metamorphosed greywacke sandstone and siltstone with minor amounts of volcanic rocks and chert (Ramp, 1975; Orr and others, 1992).

The steep slopes, high drainage density, and high gravel transport rates result from the combined effects of geologically recent uplift and erodible rock types. Analysis of uplifted 80–120 kiloannum (ka) shore platforms indicate late Quaternary uplift rates as high as 1 mm/yr (Kelsey and others, 1994), whereas geodetic and tidal observations suggest even higher historical rates of 2.5–3.5 mm/yr (Burgette and others, 2009). The rapid uplift has facilitated river incision and landsliding, especially in the upper drainage basin (Ramp, 1975).

The lower river valley, particularly along the lowermost 18 Rkm, has been strongly affected by the 130 m of sea-level rise since the culmination of the last maximum glacial period 18,000 years ago. Along the Oregon coast, rising sea levels have drowned river valleys incised during low stands of sea level, creating estuaries now extending inland from the coast. With the onset of sea-level rise, and especially during the last 2000 years of relatively stable sea level, these drowned river valleys have been filling with fluvial sediment (Komar, 1997, p. 30–32). For the Chetco River, the wide valley bottom of the lowermost 10 km is the result of this valley filling. Tidal effects extend 5 km inland, evidence that filling of the lower river valley has not yet matched Holocene sea level rise, and that the river has not yet attained a graded profile to the coast.

Hydrology

As described by early U.S. Army Corps of Engineers (1893, p. 3,431) navigation engineers, "Above the head of tide the [Chetco] river runs nearly dry in the summer, and is at all times but a small mountain stream, which becomes a torrent from the winter storms." The combination of rugged physiography, high drainage density, and high rainfall associated with a Pacific marine climate results in high annual runoff values and flashy short-duration peak flows, but very low summer flows. Average rainfall in the drainage basin is about 2.4 m (Soil Conservation Service, 1979), ranging from about 2 m/yr at Brookings and increasing with elevation to nearly 4 m/yr in the basin headwaters (Maguire, 2001, p. 116). Eighty percent of the precipitation falls during October through March, mostly resulting from 2- to 4-day Pacific frontal systems impinging from the southwest.

Flow has been measured at the USGS streamflow gaging station (14400000; Chetco River near Brookings) at FPkm 15.24 since October 1, 1969. For water years (October 1–September 30) 1970 through 2008, mean annual flow has been 64 m³/s, equating to 0.75 m of runoff from the contributing area above the measurement station. Measured annual peak flows have ranged from 280 m³/s in 2001 to 2,169 m³/s in 1996; although the 1964 peak is estimated to have been 2,420 m³/s. The mean annual peak flow is 1,085 m³/s (fig. 2).

To extend the record of peak flows to encompass the 1939–2008 analysis period, we estimated peak flows in the decades prior to 1970 on the basis of a linear regression between the Chetco River gaging station (14400000) and the USGS streamflow gaging station on the Smith River (11532500), near Crescent City in northern California and in operation since October 1931 (fig. 2A). Although the Smith River drainage basin, at 1,590 km², is 74 percent larger than the Chetco River drainage basin, both are coastal drainage basins within the Klamath Mountains physiographic province subject to similar hydrological conditions.

The reconstructed peak flow history for the Chetco River shows a pattern of increasing annual peak flows during 1931–72, with typical values ranging from 700 m³/s in the 1930s to approximately 1,400 m³/s by 1970 (fig. 2). Floods in the 1950s (particularly the 1955 peak flow event) appear similar in magnitude to the recent floods of 1971 and 2006, consistent with anecdotal records (Soil Conservation Service, 1979) that describe widespread flooding and damage associated with each of these events. Large floods with discharges exceeding 2,000 m³/s are much less common, and for the last 100 years have occurred only in 1964 and 1996, although historical records indicate similar, if not larger, peak discharges during the large regional floods of 1861 and 1890 (Maguire, 2001). The estimated peak flows for 1931–69 do not show the extremely low values (less than 500 m³/s) such as those in 1977 and 2001, although the regional drought in the 1930s coincides with generally lower annual peak flows for the period 1930-40.

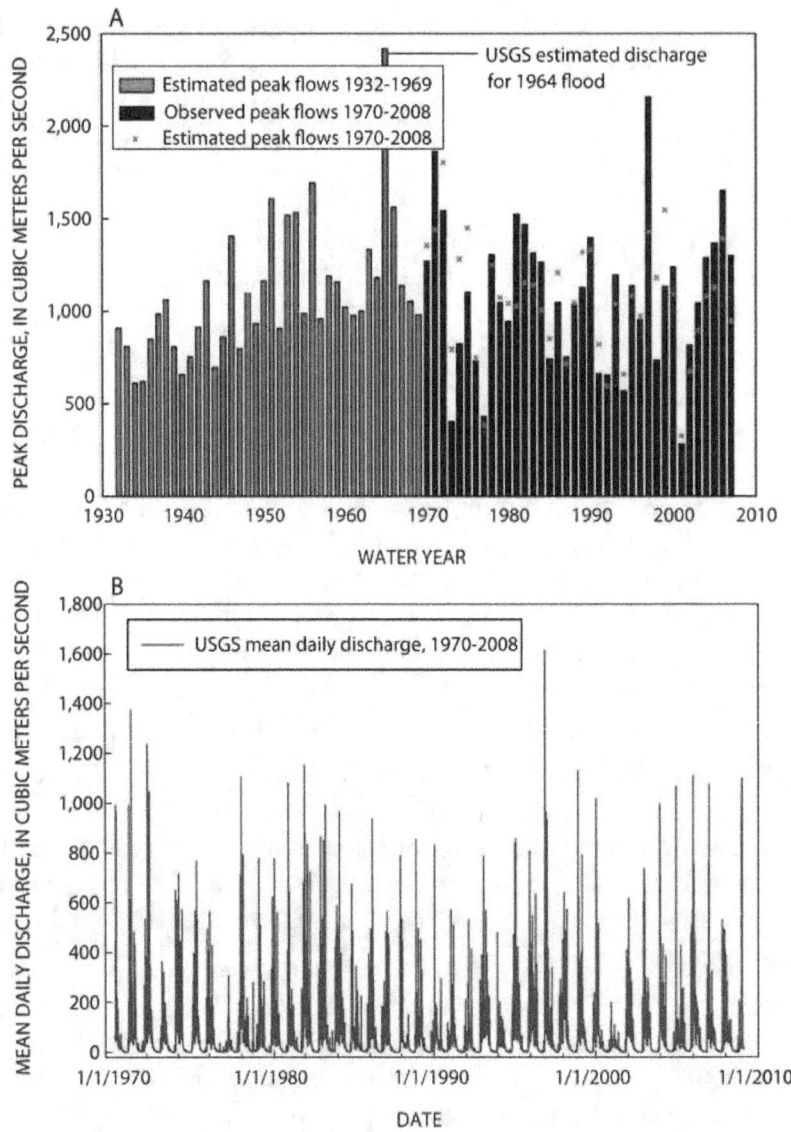

Figure 2. Graphs showing flow records for USGS streamflow gage 14400000, Chetco River near Brookings, Oregon.. A. Estimated and observed annual peak flows for water years 1930-2008. B. Mean daily discharge for water years 1970–2008. Annual peak flows; measured for water years 1971-2008, estimated for 1964 on basis of high water mark and extension of rating curve, and estimate for all other years on basis of Smith River USGS streamflow gage (11532500) in northern California. Estimates from Smith River record were determined by regression of log-transformed values on period of overlap for which *Log Chetco River Q$_{peak}$ = 0.6337 * (Log Smith River Q$_{peak}$) + 1.4708* (r = 0.83).

The Study Area

Our analysis focused on the lower 16 km of the Chetco River floodplain (fig. 1). The overall planform within the study area is that of a "wandering gravel-bed river" (Church, 1983) dominated by a single channel but also having multichanneled reaches. The channel generally alternates position against opposite valley walls, forming deep scour pools where it flows against valley walls and shallow riffles where it crosses the valley floor between large gravel bars (Klingeman, 1993). The location and general shape of many of the expansive gravel bars (fig. 3) flanking the low flow channel are fixed by the control of valley geometry on high-stage flow hydraulics and consequent patterns of erosion and deposition. Within the study reach, the low flow channel as mapped in 2008 has an average slope of 0.0012 between FPkm 16 and FPkm 4.3, and a much flatter gradient in the tidally affected lower river and estuary. The channel has a distinct pool-riffle morphology above FPkm 4.5 (fig. 4).

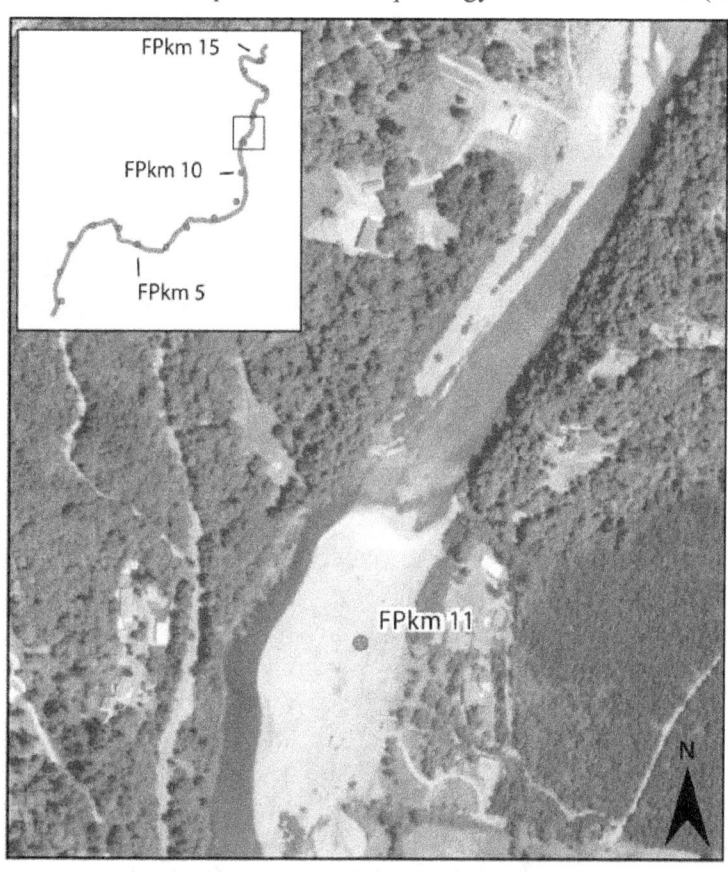

Base map modified from U.S. Department of Agriculture National Agriculture Imagery Program (NAIP) digital data.
UTM projection, Zone 10
Horizontal datum, North American Datum of 1983

```
0        100      200      300      400      500   METERS

0        400      800     1,200    1,600    2,000  FEET
```

Figure 3. Map showing example of alternate bar sequence near flood plain kilometer 11, Chetco River, Oregon. Digital orthophotograph from 2005 depicts large, channel-flanking gravel bars and low-flow channel. Flow is to the south. FPkm, floodplain kilometer.

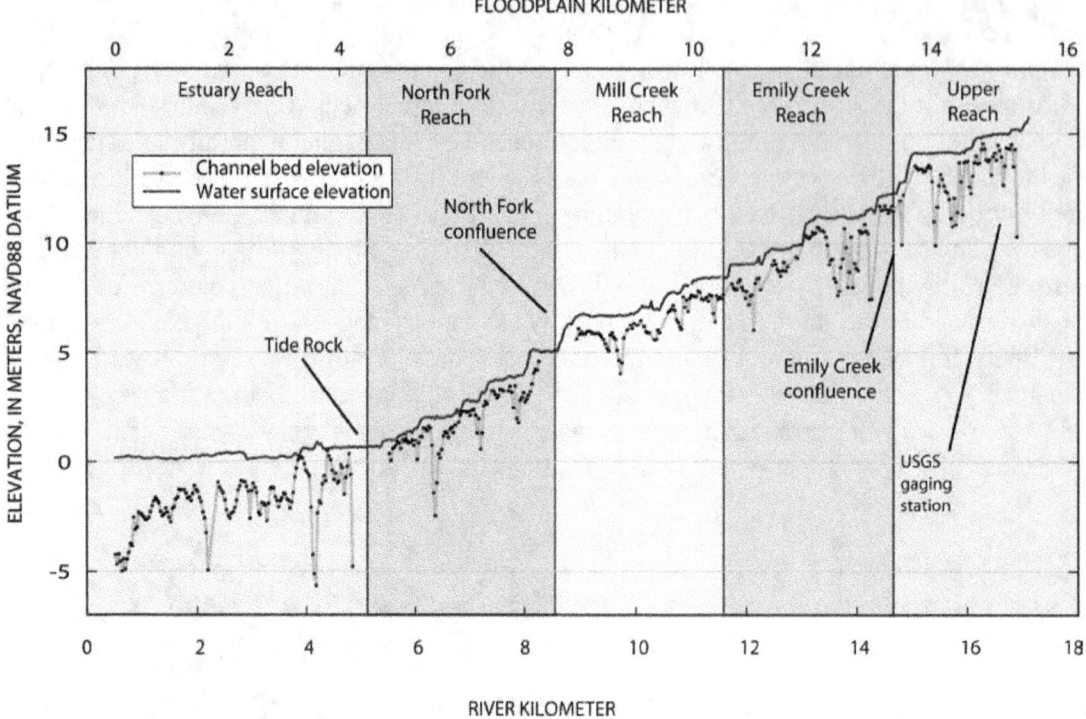

Figure 4. Graph showing water surface and bed profile along study area, Chetco River, Oregon. USGS thalweg survey during autumn 2008; water surface from LIDAR topography, flown in May–June 2008.

Longitudinal patterns in gravel transport and channel change in the study area were characterized by dividing the area into five reaches of inferred similar transport on the basis of valley geomorphology, slope, and tributary locations (figs. 1 and 4, table 1). The Upper Reach (FPkm 13.2–16) extends from the upstream end of the study area to the Emily Creek confluence, and is the most confined of all five reaches with an average floodplain width of 215 m. The valley and channel widen slightly through the Emily Creek Reach (extending between the confluences of Emily Creek and Mill Creek, FPkm 13.2–10.6). The Mill Creek Reach (FPkm 10.6–7.6) encompasses the transition from the more stable upper reaches to the wider, more dynamic lower reaches, with floodplain width increasing to 800 m as the Chetco River approaches its confluence with the North Fork of the Chetco River. The valley is widest along the lower portion of the Mill Creek Reach and the North Fork Reach (FPkm 7.6–4.3), before narrowing and abruptly flattening as it enters the Estuary Reach, which corresponds to the tidally influenced zone from FPkm 4.3 (near the prominent local landmark of Tide Rock) to the mouth of the Chetco River (FPkm 0).

Table 1. Summary of reach attributes for the study area, Chetco River, Oregon.

[Abbreviations: m, meter; FPkm, floodplain kilometer]

Reach name	Distance along floodplain axis	General description	Average water surface slope (2008) (m/m)	Average floodplain width (m)	Average width of low-flow channel (2008) (m)	Instream gravel extraction sites 1995-2008
Upper Reach	FPkm 13.2– FPkm 16	Steep, narrow channel corridor where channel and gravel bars have remained fairly stable over time	0.00138	213	45	Fitzhugh Bar (FPkm 15.4), operated by Tidewater Contractors Inc.
Emily Creek Reach	FPkm 10.6– FPkm 13.2	Similar planform and stability as Upper Reach, but wider valley bottom and increasing bar size.	0.00109	285	48	Tamba Bar (FPkm 11), operated by South Coast Lumber Co.
Mill Creek Reach	FPkm 7.6– FPkm 10.6	Transition reach between the stable upper reaches and more dynamic North Fork Reach	0.00072	474	56	-
North Fork Reach	FPkm 4.3– FPkm 7.6	Historically most dynamic of all reaches. Extensive in-stream gravel mining at multiple sites since 1930s.	0.00140	343	47	North Fork site (FPkm 7– 7.8), operated by Freeman Rock Inc.
Estuary Reach	FPkm 0– FPkm 4.3	Tidally influenced, confined between steep valley walls. Mouth of river historically was historically dynamic but navigation improvements have stablized channel entrance. Extensive gravel mining along multiple sites prior to 1990s.	0.00015	329	96	Estuary Bar (FPkm 2.8), operated by Tidewater Contractors Inc.

Land-Use and Landscape Disturbance in the Chetco River Basin

Because of its rugged topography and remote location, the Chetco River basin was largely uninhabited until the early 20th century, and even today most of the drainage basin is publically owned and managed as forest lands and wilderness. Late in the 19th century, the U.S. Army Corps of Engineers (1893, p. 3,432) reported that "probably not over 100 people living in the whole Chetco Valley." By the 1930s, individuals and lumber companies were logging on private lands along tributary valleys in the lower drainage basin (Chetco Watershed Council, 1995). Logging activity expanded to the upper basin during the peak harvest period of the 1950s–1960s and then steadily declined through the 1990s (John P. Williams, U.S. Department of Agriculture Forest Service, written commun., April 28, 2009). As of 2001, 97 percent of the Chetco River basin is managed as forest lands and wilderness by the U.S. Forest Service (USFS), Bureau of Land Management (BLM), and to a lesser extent, private timber companies

(Maguire, 2001). More than half of the basin (521 km^2), including much of the headwaters, is in the Kalmiopis Wilderness Area. Other important land uses in the middle and lower basin include agriculture, rural residential development, and gravel quarries, which in total cover 2 percent of the total basin area, whereas urban areas near the mouth of the Chetco River occupy only 1 percent of the basin (Maguire, 2001).

Forest Management and Fire

Although a variety of natural and anthropogenic disturbances may influence channel conditions along the Chetco River, those likely to have the greatest effect in terms of sediment transport and channel planform along the study are watershed-scale disturbances such as floods, logging (and related) activities, forest fires; and activities within the study reach, including navigation improvements to the estuary, development and bank protection, and instream gravel mining. Logging and associated road building can increase peak flows (Wemple and others, 1996; Jones and Grant, 1996, 2001; Bowling and others, 2000) and the frequency of landslides (Kelsey and others, 1995), resulting in sedimentation along lower reaches of affected basins (Madej, 1995). Although data describing historical logging practices, road building, and resultant landscape change are sparse for the Chetco River, it is possible that the period of peak logging in the 1950s–1960s may have affected sediment influx into the lower Chetco River.

In recent decades, two large regional fires burned portions of the upper Chetco basin. The Biscuit Fire of summer 2002 was one of the largest historical forest fires in the Klamath Mountains, burning more than 57 percent of the Chetco River drainage basin with varying severity. In many places within the upper drainage basin, the Biscuit Fire overlapped with areas previously burned by the 1987 Silver Fire, although the Silver Fire only burned 10 percent of the basin (U.S. Forest Service, 2008). Possible long-term effects on Chetco River channel conditions resulting from the Biscuit Fire include enhanced runoff and erosion resulting from loss of vegetation (U.S. Forest Service and Bureau of Land Management, 2004), leading to downstream sedimentation.

Navigation Improvements

The Chetco River estuary is one of the smallest estuaries in Oregon, with a tidal prism extending only 4.6 km upstream from the Pacific Ocean, and its lateral extent constrained between steep valley walls (Ratti and Kraeg, 1979). Although the U.S. Army Corps of Engineers (1893, p. 3,431) originally declared that "the Chetco River estuary was unworthy of improvement" because of its small size and lack of regional commerce, expansion of the wood products industry and commercial fishing resulted in authorization of a series of navigational improvements as part of the 1945 River and Harbor Act (Slotta and Tang, 1976; Ratti and Kraeg, 1979). By 1959, a pair of jetties had been constructed at the mouth of the river, and an entrance channel dredged through the bar that had historically blocked seasonal entrance to the estuary. Navigation and harbor improvements continued through the 1960s and 1970s, with the dredging of two boat basins in former tidelands areas and construction of a protective dike (Slotta and Tang, 1976; Ratti and Kraeg, 1979). These alterations were accompanied by filling of a historical lagoon by the Port of Brookings to reduce flooding and improve access to the moorages (Oregon Department of State Lands, 1972).

Since the early 1960s, the U.S. Army Corps of Engineers dredged each year to maintain the entrance to the Chetco River channel, removing an average of 22,000 m^3/yr (Judy Linton, U.S. Army Corps of Engineers, written commun. February 23, 2009; fig. 5). Only part of this dredged volume, however, is removed from the lowermost kilometer of the Chetco River, with the balance removed downstream of the jetties at the entrance to the channel. Additionally, it is uncertain how much of this dredged sediment, even that within the lowermost river, is derived from downstream river transport rather than marine transport into the lower Chetco River. For similar Oregon estuaries of the Yaquina and Alsea Rivers, most sand at the river mouth is of marine origin (Kulm and Byrne, 1966; Peterson and others, 1982). For the similarly sized (725 km^2) Redwood Creek in northern California, Ricks (1995) showed that the sand in the estuary has a composition more similar to nearby Pacific beaches than that from the Redwood Creek drainage basin, indicating that a substantial portion of the Redwood Creek estuary sand is from marine transport into the estuary.

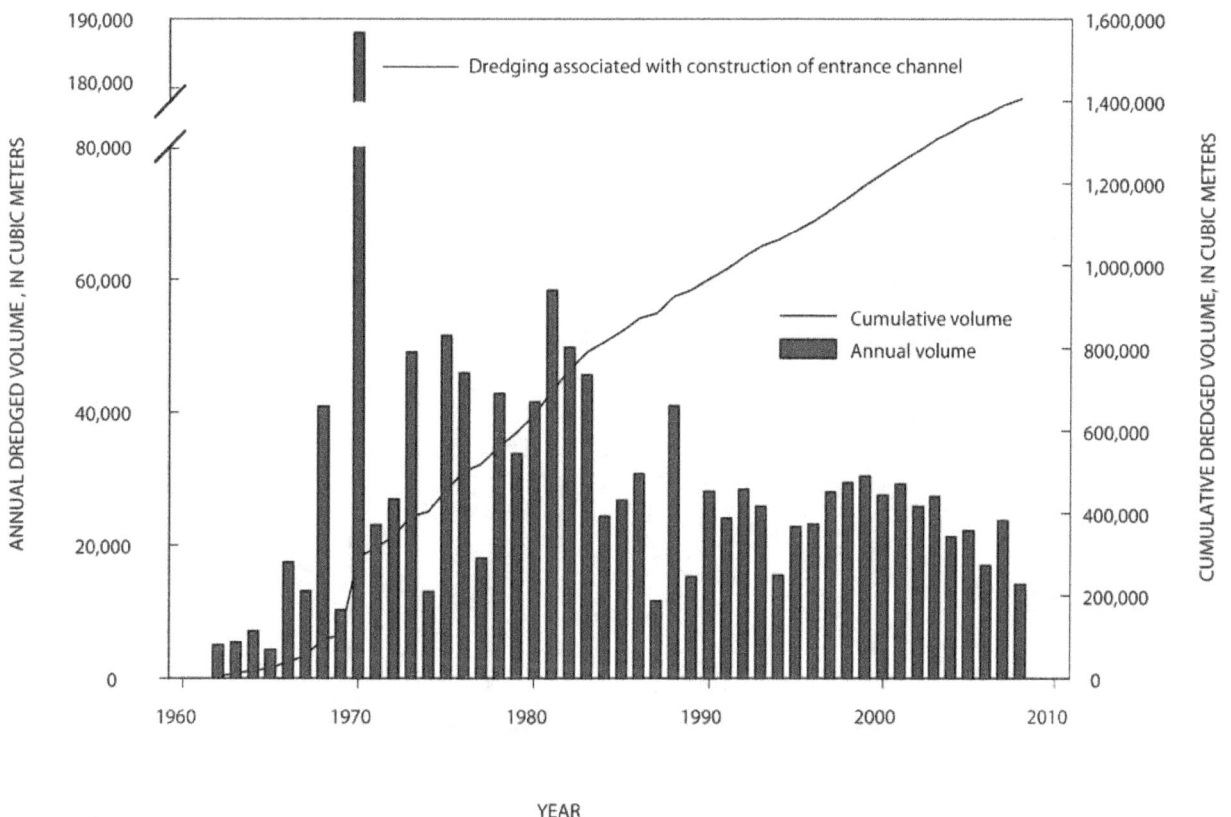

YEAR

Figure 5. Graph showing annual navigational dredging volumes, 1962-2008, Chetco River, Oregon. Dredging began in 1962 and maintains navigation clearance at the river mouth and the boat basin. Data source: Judy Linton, U.S. Army Corps of Engineers, written commun., February 23, 2009.

Chetco River Gravel Mining

Sand and gravel has been mined for aggregate from bars flanking the low flow channel of the Chetco River floodplain for nearly a century. All of this removal has been downstream of FPkm 16 and has primarily been in the estuary and near the confluence of the North Fork Chetco River at FPkm 7.5. Although historical records of removal volumes and practices are incomplete, accounts from long-time residents indicate that gravel extraction began in the early 1900s when gravel was removed by drag line from the estuary, and by the 1930s, several bars below FPkm 7.5 were being mined (T. Freeman, Freeman Rock Inc., written commun., 2009). Prior to 1967, no permit was required for instream gravel extraction in the State of Oregon, and on many rivers, it was common for aggregate to be removed from deep pits that extended well below the water line. Although anecdotal accounts (M. McCabe, Oregon Department of State Lands, oral commun., 2009; T. Freeman, Freeman Rock Inc., oral commun., 2009) indicate that several operators utilized such pits along the lower Chetco River, and aerial photographs from the 1930s to 1960s show possible water-filled pits on gravel bars below FPkm 6, there are no records to better describe or quantify the volume of mining from this time period. After the 1960s, pit extraction was gradually replaced with bar "scalping" or "skimming" techniques using scrapers or other heavy equipment to remove only the surface of the gravel bar, typically to an elevation close to the low-flow water level.

On the Chetco River, removal of instream gravel for aggregate probably peaked in the 1970s and 1980s, when there were at least 15 instream gravel operators within the study area and removal volumes were much higher than during recent years. Records listing removal volumes from a small number of operators show that average annual extraction for the period 1976–1980 was approximately 140,000 m^3/yr (Marquess and Associates, 1980), a rate three times greater than that for 1993–2008 (fig. 6). In 1994, the Chetco River was declared navigable (and hence publicly owned) by the State of Oregon, and royalty fees were assessed on instream gravel extraction. Largely in response to tighter permitting conditions and fees, only three companies have continued commercial gravel extraction on the Chetco River, and the annual volume of gravel removal has declined substantially. From 1995 through 2008, instream gravel was mined at four primary sites along the Chetco River:

- Tidewater Estuary Bar (FPkm 3), operated by Tidewater Contractors Inc.
- Freeman North Fork Site (FPkm 7.5), operated by Freeman Rock Inc.
- Tamba Bar (FPkm 11), operated by South Coast Lumber Co.
- Fitzhugh Bar (FPkm 15.5), operated by Tidewater Contractors Inc.

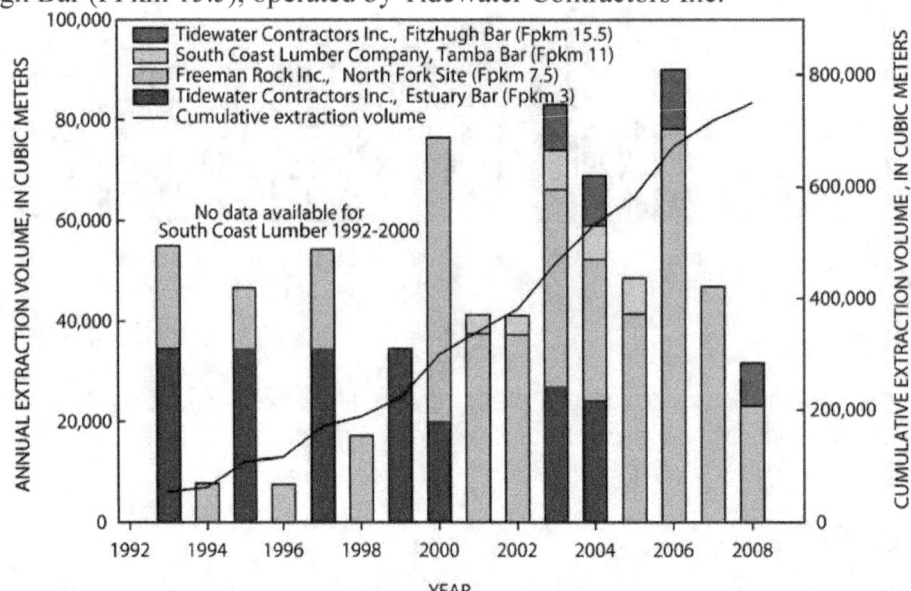

Figure 6. Graph showing instream commercial gravel mining, Chetco River, Oregon, 1993–2008. Values reported by commercial operators and corroborated with records of Oregon Department of State Lands. Values for Estuary Bar for 1993–1999 are estimates provided by Robert Elayer (Tidewater Contractors Inc, written commun., 2008).

Information provided by the gravel operators for mined volumes between 2000 and 2008 (the period for which actual extraction volumes for all operators is available) indicate that on average, nearly 59,000 m^3 of aggregate was removed annually between the three operators, with year-to-year values ranging between 32,000 m^3 (2008) to 90,000 m^3 (2006) depending on permit conditions and gravel replenishment at mining sites (fig. 6).

Valley Bottom Mapping and Analysis of Historical Channel Change

Historical and current channel maps, surveys, and aerial photographs provide a means for assessing planform and vertical changes to the Chetco River study area since the late 1930s. In this study, we document planform changes to the morphology and land-cover types of the valley bottom by analysis of multiple sets of aerial photographs dating back to 1939. Vertical changes to the channel and floodplain were assessed from sparser historical data, including 1939 and 1977 surveys, and the record of channel geometry documented at the USGS streamflow measurement station at FPkm 15.2. Current information on topography, bathymetry, and vegetation was based on (1) LIDAR topography acquired in spring 2008 and provided by the Oregon LIDAR Consortium (Oregon Department of Geology and Mineral Industries, 2009), (2) channels and estuaries surveyed in summer 2008, and (3) half-meter orthoimagery for 2005 developed from summer 2005 aerial photographs as part of the U.S. Department of Agriculture National Agriculture Imagery Program (NAIP).

Historical Changes in Channel Planform and Vegetation

Planview changes in channel morphology were quantified by mapping channel features from eight time periods using aerial photographs and the LIDAR. The time periods selected for channel mapping were chosen to track channel change for the longest possible time period and to serve as a basis for assessing erosion and deposition for five time intervals: 1939–43, 1962–65, 1995–2000, 2000–2005, and 2005–08. These times were chosen on the basis of photo availability and quality, as well as to encompass specific events possibly affecting channel morphology. The period 1939–43 represents a period of minimal land use in the Chetco River basin and little gravel extraction. The period 1962-65 includes the 1964 flood of record and also represents an era of increasing land use throughout the basin, including navigational improvements near the mouth of the Chetco River and increased gravel extraction along the lower river corridor and timber harvest within the drainage basin. The three recent time periods (1995–2000, 2000–2005 and 2005–08) postdate the era of most voluminous gravel extraction and timber harvest but encompass the two large floods of 1996 and 2006.

Acquisition and Rectification of Historical Aerial Photographs

Digital orthoimagery from 1995, 2000, and 2005 have been previously rectified and georeferenced and are in the public domain (table 2). By contrast, older sets of aerial photographs were available only as paper prints or negatives and required scanning, georeferencing, and rectification as part of this study (table 2). Coverage was complete for the entire study area for all photograph sets except for the photos from 1939 which extended only up to FPkm 13.5, leaving the upstream 2.5 km without coverage for 1939. The aerial photographs and LIDAR were all acquired during flows less than 15 m^3/s, well within the low-flow channel (tables 2 and 3).

Table 2. Aerial photographs and orthophotographs used in the sediment transport study, Chetco River, Oregon

[**Abbreviations:** m³/s, cubic meters per second; FPkm, floodplain kilometer; USACE, U.S. Army Corps of Engineers; USFS, U.S. Forest Service; USDA, U.S. Department of Agriculture; USGS, U.S. Geological Survey; NAIP, National Agriculture Imagery Program. * Indicates estimated discharge, calculated by extending the Chetco River USGS streamflow gage data based on data from the Smith River USGS gage.]

Year	Original format	Coverage	Flight date	Approximate discharge at photo date (m³/s)	Photo scale or orthophoto resolution	Original source	Rectification source
1939	Aerial photograph	FPkm 0-13	5/27/1939	11*	1:10,200	USACE	This study
1943	Aerial photograph	FPkm 0–16	8/3–8/4/1943	5*	1:40,000	USFS	This study
1962	Aerial photograph	FPkm 0–16	7/18/1962 for FPkm 0–4.5, 6/7/1962 for FPkm 4.5–16	11* (FPkm 4.5–16), 4* (FPkm 0–4.5)	1:8,800	South Coast Lumber Company	This study
1965	Aerial photograph	FPkm 0–16	6/22/1965	7*	1:20,000	USDA	This study
1995	Orthophotograph	FPkm 0–16	5/27/1995	15	1 pixel = 1 m	USGS	USGS
2000	Orthophotograph	FPkm 0–16	7/27/2000–8/14/2000	3–4	1 pixel = 1 m	USGS	USGS
2005	Orthophotograph	FPkm 0–16	7/17/2005	9	1 pixel = 1 m	NAIP	NAIP

Table 3. Map and survey data reviewed in the sediment transport study, Chetco River, Oregon

[**Abbreviations:** FPkm, floodplain kilometer; USACE, U.S. Army Corps of Engineers; USGS, U.S. Geological Survey; GLO, General Land Office; SCS, Soil Conservation Service; LiDAR, light detection and ranging; GIS, geographic information system]

Original Source for map or survey	Type of map or survey	Date of map or survey	Date(s) survey was performed	Coverage	Comments
USACE	Navigational bathymetry map	1939	June 20–July 14, 1939	FPkm 0–4.5	Scanned, rectified and digitized by USGS staff using 1939 aerial photographs.
GLO	Township survey	1879	September 16–October 2, 1845 and February 25–March 12, 1879	FPkm 3–11.5	Survey to delineate township and section lines; channel and gravel bar locations were surveyed at the section boundaries, with intervening areas approximated.

Table 3. Map and survey data reviewed in the sediment transport study, Chetco River, Oregon—continued

[**Abbreviations:** FPkm, floodplain kilometer; USACE, U.S. Army Corps of Engineers; USGS, U.S. Geological Survey; GLO, General Land Office; SCS, Soil Conservation Service; LiDAR, light detection and ranging; GIS, geographic information system]

SCS	Flood study	1979	1977	FPkm 0–16	Cross sections converted to NAVD 88 vertical datum (this study) for comparison with 2008 data
Watershed Sciences, Inc.	LiDAR survey	Expected release in 2009	May 3–July 6, 2008	FPkm 0–16	Discharge during LiDAR flight ranged from approximately 37 m^3/sec.
USGS	Bathyemetric survey	This study	September 16 and 17, 2008	FPkm 0–3.5	Bathymetric survey of Chetco River estuary using Echosounder to produce 3–5 depth measurements per meter of survey line.
USGS	Cross-section and long profile survey	This study	October 7–9, 2008	FPkm 3–16	See accompanying GIS layers and metadata for map and survey descriptions

Full details of georeferencing and rectifying are included in the metadata for the GIS maps prepared in conjunction with this study (U.S. Geological Survey, 2009), but to summarize: The scanned historical aerial photographs were georeferenced in ArcGIS 9.2 using the orthophotographs from 2005 as a base layer and following the methodology of Hughes and others (2006). For the photographs from 1943, 1962, and 1965, we acquired 6–16 ground control points per photograph, preferentially located near the channel. A second order polynomial fit was applied to georeference the photographs, providing root mean square error (RMSE) values ranging from approximately 1 to 4.4 m. The photography from 1939 was more difficult to register because of the small area covered by each photograph (approximately 1.5 x 2 km) and the small number of feature points present in the photographs from 1939 and 2005. Consequently, the photographs from 1939 were georeferenced using only 3–6 ground control points per photograph and rectified using a first order polynomial, which resulted in RMSE values of 0.35–3.6 m. Once georeferenced, each photograph was rectified and then combined to create a seamless mosaic of images for each period.

Uncertainties and Limitations to Planimetric Mapping

Even with established protocols and spatial analysis techniques, uncertainty and error result from interpretive mapping of land-surface features from aerial photographs of varying quality and light conditions and from different time periods (Gurnell, 1997; Mount and Louis, 2005; Hughes and others, 2006). For this study, the quality and resolution of the photographs varied both spatially and temporally but was sufficient for most of our mapping objectives. The major source of mapping error for most features in this study resulted from imprecise registration and rectification of historical aerial photographs, especially for the older photos for which there were few features to use as control points. The RMSE values indicate that horizontal position uncertainties are less than 5 m; however, from test trials, we more conservatively judge positional errors for the historical aerial photographs resulting from the georeferencing and rectification process to be almost everywhere less than 20 m. Positional errors associated with the publicly available orthophotographs for 1995, 2000, and 2005 are less than 6 m. Georeferencing errors will have their greatest effect on analyses of photo-to-photo change, such as for quantitative estimates of channel movement and bar growth and erosion, but will have little influence on measurements of total areas of features such as the for the channel and gravel bars.

Another important consideration in comparing mapped features from different time periods is differences in discharge between aerial photograph sets. Although all photography and LIDAR were acquired during low-flow periods (tables 2 and 3), small changes in discharge can influence delineation of channel and bar areas, particularly in areas where the channel is wide and shallow. We partly account for this in some analyses by determining the relations of bar and channel area to flow on the basis of a one-dimensional hydraulic model and the channel and floodplain topography for 2008 (see complete model description in the Hydraulic Modeling section below). This relation (fig. 7), which indicates that as much as 15 percent of the total bar area is inundated within the range of flows in the analyzed photographs, was used to normalize the channel width and bar area measurements for all analysis periods to a constant discharge of 2.8 m^3/s, a discharge slightly less than the lowest discharge associated with any of the photography sets.

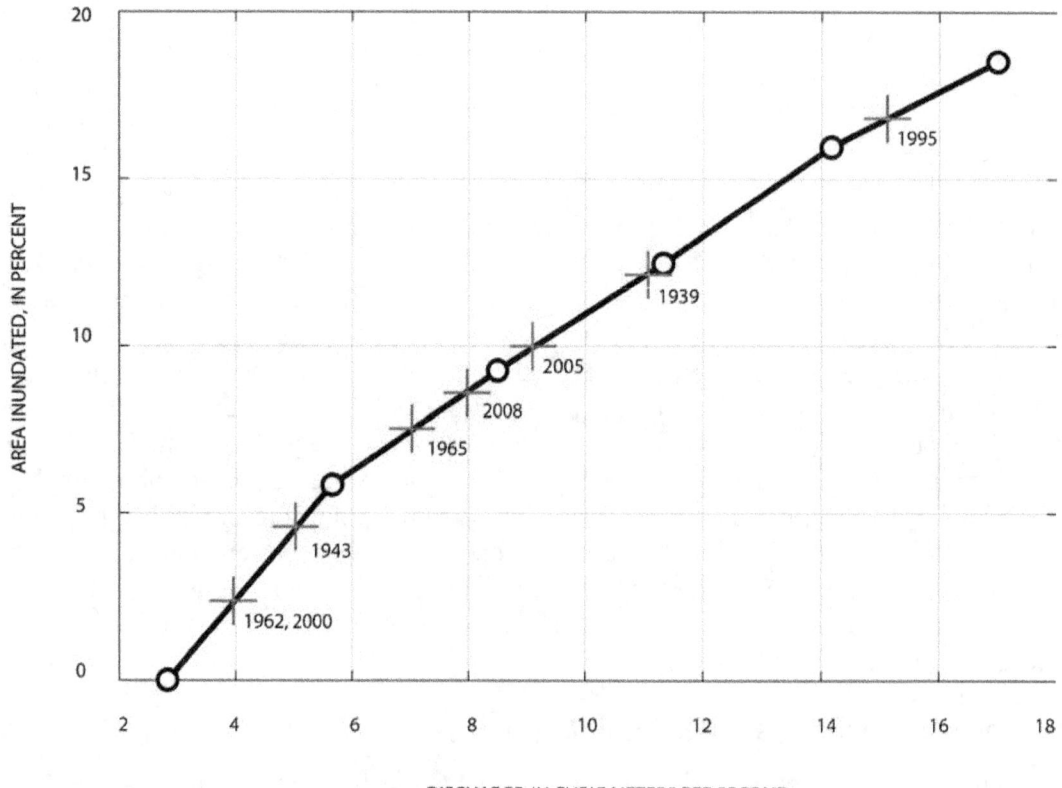

Figure 7. Graph showing relation of bar inundation with discharge, Chetco River, Oregon. Area inundated for each discharge was calculated on the basis of six modeled discharges between 2.8 and 17 cubic meters per second and overlaying corresponding inundated areas onto mapped bar areas. This relation was used to normalize bar and channel measurements from different photo sets to a common discharge of 2.8 cubic meters per second. Also shown are discharges for the seven photo sets and the LIDAR.

Tide level has an especially large influence on the mapping within the Estuary Reach, particularly for gravel bars submerged with each tidal cycle. Because tidal stage did vary between photography sets, we mapped only the portion of bars inferred to be above tidal range during low flow periods. This was possible because bars subject to daily tidal inundation have significant algal growth, giving them a distinctly darker tint in the photographs. The tidally inundated portions of the bars were included in the primary channel map unit.

In summary, considering registration errors and digitizing precision, we infer the horizontal uncertainty of the digital channel and floodplain maps to be less than 15 m for sharply defined features. For the maps from 1995 to 2008, positional uncertainty is probably less than 6 m as judged by the precise agreement between persistent features observable on this imagery. Flow variations between photography sets add additional uncertainty, but this can in part be accounted for by normalizing bar and channel area measurements to a reference discharge.

Mapping Channel Features, Floodplain Vegetation, and Bank Materials

The photograph mosaics provide the basis for systematic mapping of channels and bars, as well as broadscale land-cover and vegetation characteristics. Geomorphic features were mapped for each of the seven photography sets and from the LIDAR. The mapped features form a foundation for evaluating changes to channel and bar planform and support the analysis of depositional and erosional volumes described later in this report. Land cover and vegetation was mapped for only the photographs from 1939, 1962, 1965, and 2005 in order determine coarse patterns of change in vegetation cover and density within the geologic floodplain.

Mapping of geomorphic features was confined to the active channel, defined as the area typically inundated during annual high flows as judged by the presence of water and flow-modified surfaces (Church, 1988). Features within the active channel were divided into mapping units: (1) primary (low flow) channel, (2) gravel bars, (3) alcoves (side channels or other wetted areas connected to the primary channel), (4) tributaries, (5) jetties, (6) disconnected water features, and (7) the constructed boat basin. For each time period, all such features larger than about 200 m^2 were digitized at a scale of 1:1,000. All linework was reviewed at a scale of 1:3,000 by another project team member to ensure consistency between time periods.

The primary channel was mapped by digitizing the wetted perimeter of the main channel as shown on aerial photographs and the LIDAR topography. Gravel bars, defined as gravel-covered surfaces with evidence of recent mobilization (bare or sparse vegetation) were separated into two categories: floodplain bars (sharing a margin with the floodplain) and island bars (completely surrounded by water). Tributary channels and tributary fans were also mapped where these features were discernable; however, due to differences in photograph resolution and vegetation, tributary features present in certain time periods were not always apparent in others. Disconnected water features were defined as any water body within the active channel area completely separated from other water features, and mostly consisted of ponds in swales on floodplain bars. Constructed features consisted of the boat basin, jetties, and the dike alongside the boat basin.

Although geomorphic features were mapped for only the active channel corridor, basic land-cover attributes, including vegetation, were mapped for the entire geomorphic floodplain, but for only four time periods. The geomorphic floodplain was defined for this study as the relatively flat surface formed of recent alluvium occupying the valley bottom, and was mapped on the basis of topography and field inspection. The floodplain boundaries depicted here do not necessarily correspond to inundation levels of specific flood discharges or flood frequency. Choices of map units for the land cover and vegetation mapping were based on review of historical and recent aerial photographs to ensure that each of the land cover classes could be distinguished from each set of photographs, supplemented by field inspections during September 2008. Species information was compiled from field manuals and with assistance from silviculturist Robyn Darbyshire (U.S. Department of Agriculture Forest Service, oral commun., September 12, 2008).

Eight mappable classes of land cover were defined, with three of these classes also assigned vegetation density ranges. Detailed descriptions of each mapping category are provided in the metadata accompanying the GIS files (U.S. Geological Survey, 2009) and are only summarized here: All wetted features, including the primary channel and alcoves, are mapped as *Water*, whereas rocky outcrops, including "Tide Rock" and "Morris Rock" (fig. 1), are mapped as *Bedrock*. Major paved roads, as well as developments and clusters of houses are mapped as *Developed* areas, though individual houses and small dirt roads are classified according to the surrounding land cover. *Bare* surfaces are nonbedrock terrestrial surfaces with less than 25 percent cover of discernable vegetation, typically appearing very light colored on aerial photographs. These are chiefly gravel bars with recently disturbed surfaces (fig. 8). *Sparse Vegetation* is the designation for surfaces with 5–25 percent vegetative cover, and typically consists of isolated trees, grasses, and shrubs. These areas are also almost always gravel bars vegetated with early successional species (fig. 8). Grasses, lawns, agricultural lands, and various herbaceous communities (including *Vetch* spp., *Bacharis* spp., and members of the composite family) are mapped as *Herbaceous Vegetation*, which has smooth texture and light brown or gray color in the aerial photographs (fig. 8). The *Woody Shrub* mapping unit is for areas with low canopies (chiefly less than 5 m) sufficiently dense to appear relatively smooth in the aerial photographs. Woody shrub cover is typically composed of willows (*Salix* spp.) and small (less than 5 m tall) alders (*Alnus* spp.). This type is found almost exclusively on gravel bars, commonly growing in narrow groves or thickets aligned parallel to the channel (fig. 8). Clusters of large trees are mapped as *Mature Trees*, and typically included black cottonwood (*Populous balsamifera*), myrtlewood *(Umbellularia californica),* and tall alders on floodplain surfaces outside of the active channel area (fig. 8). Although mature trees typically had a distinct size and texture when compared against willows and other shrub-type vegetation in the aerial photographs, it was difficult to discern small trees from willows; hence, canopies associated with trees less than about 5 m tall were grouped together in the *Woody Shrub* category. Vegetation density values of moderate (25–75 percent cover) and dense (75–100 percent cover) were assigned to *Herbaceous, Woody Shrub,* and *Mature Tree* mapping units.

Figure 8. Photographs showing examples of landcover mapping categories, as depicted in an orthophotograph from 2005 and oblique photographs near floodplain kilometer 9 of the Chetco River, Oregon. Land cover was mapped from aerial photographs and included five vegetation categories: *Bare, Sparse Vegetation, Herbaceous Vegetation, Woody Shrub,* and *Mature Trees.* (Photographs by Scott Anderson, U.S. Geological Survey, September, 2008.)

The bank materials along the Chetco River corridor were mapped in such a manner as to differentiate reaches bordered by erodible sediments from reaches flanked by more resistant bedrock or artificial revetment. Bank materials were defined as the natural or artificial material bordering the active channel and were mapped by walking the length of the study area and recording the condition and composition of the channel banks. Field observations were then compared with the recent orthoimagery and LIDAR topography to construct continuous maps of bank materials along both edges of the active channel at a scale of 1:5,000. The map units include the primary types of bank materials: (1) floodplain risers formed of erodible sand and gravel contained in fluvial deposits flanking the active channel, (2) bedrock outcrops, and (3) artificial fill (primarily consisting of material used to fill the former tidelands near the present location of the boat basin at FPkm 0). Bank protection revetment, chiefly consisting of large angular boulders, was mapped as an overlay to the three primary categories of bank material.

Results of Channel Mapping

Evident overall trends for 1939-2008 for active-channel features of the study reach are a 34 percent reduction in gravel bar area and a slight decrease in channel sinuosity (fig. 9). Channel width has not changed systematically over this time period. The reduction in bar area is much greater than can be attributed to differences in flow stage between photo sets (figs. 9 and 10). These overall changes, however, reflect a temporally and spatially varied history of channel behavior. The largest change, the decrease in bar area, is almost entirely accounted by the large reduction in floodplain bar surfaces between 1965 and 1995. Prior to 1965 and subsequent to 1995, bar areas may have increased slightly for some reaches, especially between 2005 and 2008, although at rates small relative to uncertainties mapping and the effects of the different discharges on mapped areas (figs. 9 and 10).

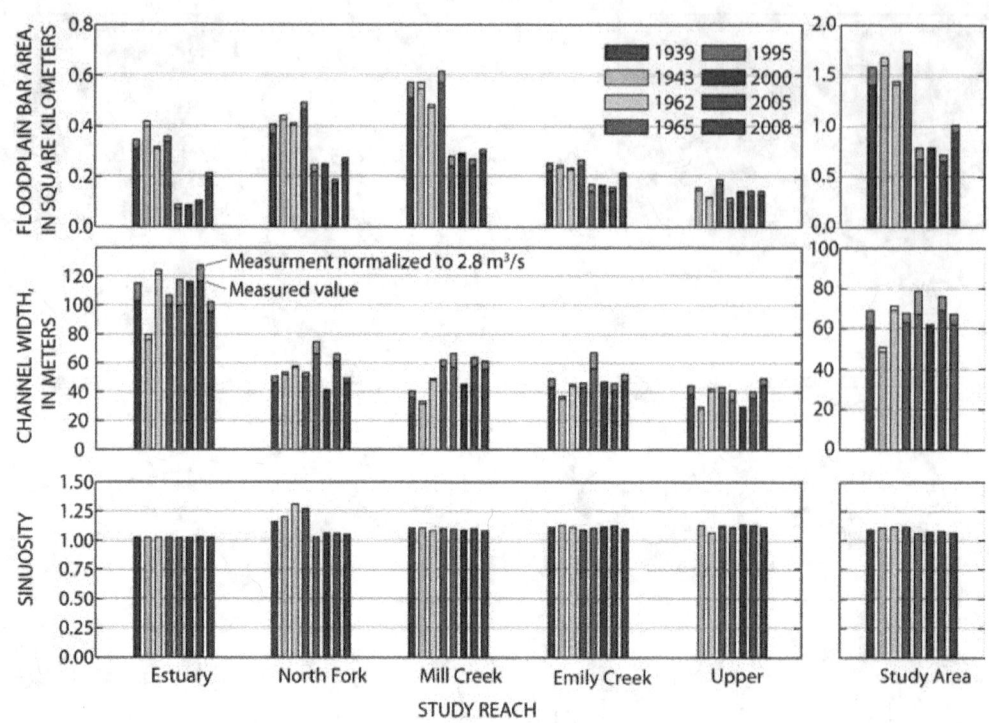

Figure 9. Graphs showing summary of channel change during 1939–2008 for Chetco River, Oregon, study area. The 1939 photographs only partly cover the Upper Reach; hence there are no 1939 measurements for bar area and sinuosity for that reach, and channel width is only a partial measurement.

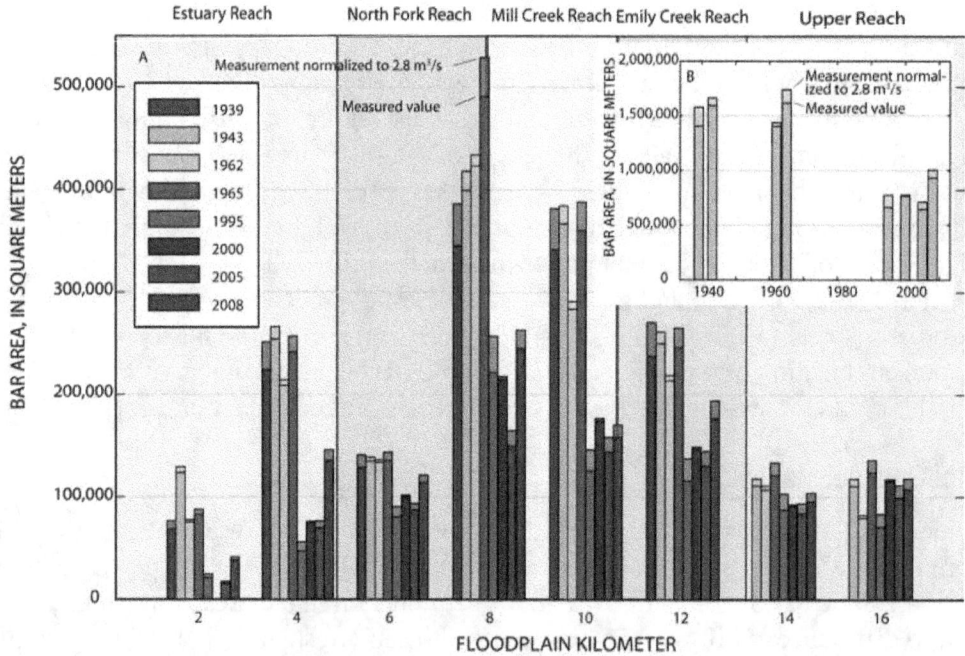

Figure 10. Graph showing spatial and temporal variation in gravel bar area for eight locations along the Chetco River, Oregon, 1939-2008. A. Aggregated by 2-kilometer-long lengths of floodplain. No data for 1939 upstream from floodplain kilometer 13. B. For total study reach.

Historical channel change for 1939–2008 along the Chetco River was greatest along the lower reaches where the valley bottom is wide and a greater percentage of the channel is bordered by more erodible floodplain materials (figs. 11–15). The North Fork (fig. 13) and lower Mill Creek (fig. 14) Reaches have had the most planform change. For the North Fork Reach, the 1939 channel was relatively sinuous and narrow, with a sinuosity of 1.16 and an average width of 47 m. The maps from 1995 to 2008 show the channel to be straighter, with a sinuosity in 2008 of 1.05. In conjunction with sinuosity changes, the average water-surface slope of the North Fork Reach has increased by about 10 percent between 1939 and 2008, from 0.000767 m/m to 0.000849 m/m. Low-flow channel width changes have been more variable; for example, reach average width along the North Fork Reach was 66 m in 1995, 41 m in 2000, 61 m in 2005, and had decreased to 47 m by 2008 (fig. 9). Between 1939 and 2008, normalized (for flow stage) total bar area for the North Fork Reach diminished from 400,000 m^2 to 270,000 m^2 (fig. 9). Similarly, bar area for the Mill Creek Reach has been reduced from 600,000 m^2 in 1939 to about 300,000 m^2 in 2008 (fig. 9). The net changes for these reaches, however, do not reflect continuous trends as there have been episodes of increases in sinuosity and bar area within the overall record (figs. 9 and 10).

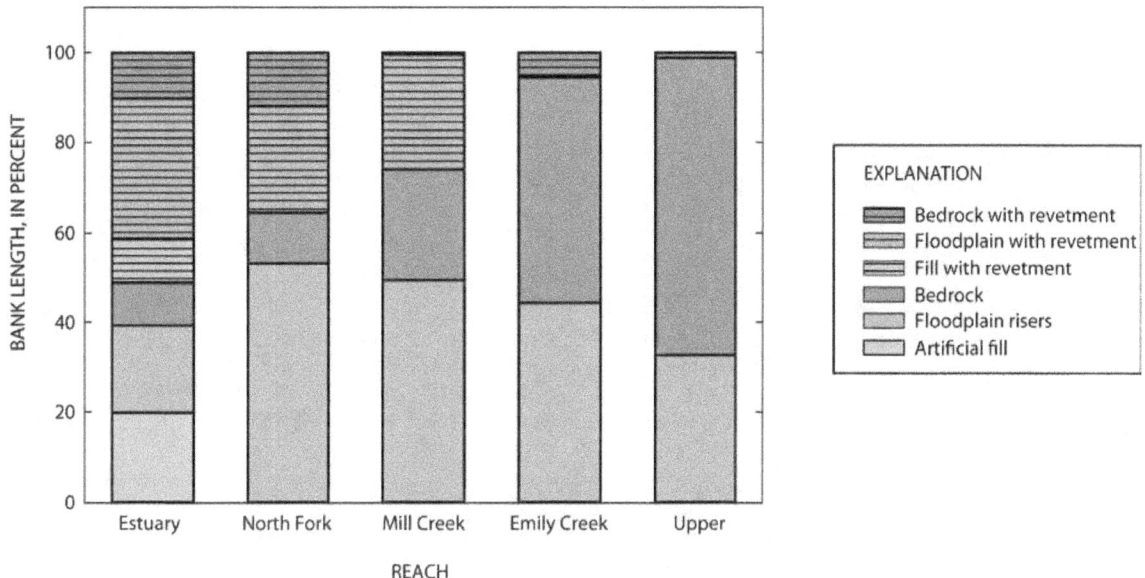

Figure 11. Graph showing reach segregated distribution of bank material and revetment between floodplain kilometer 0 and 16, Chetco River, Oregon.

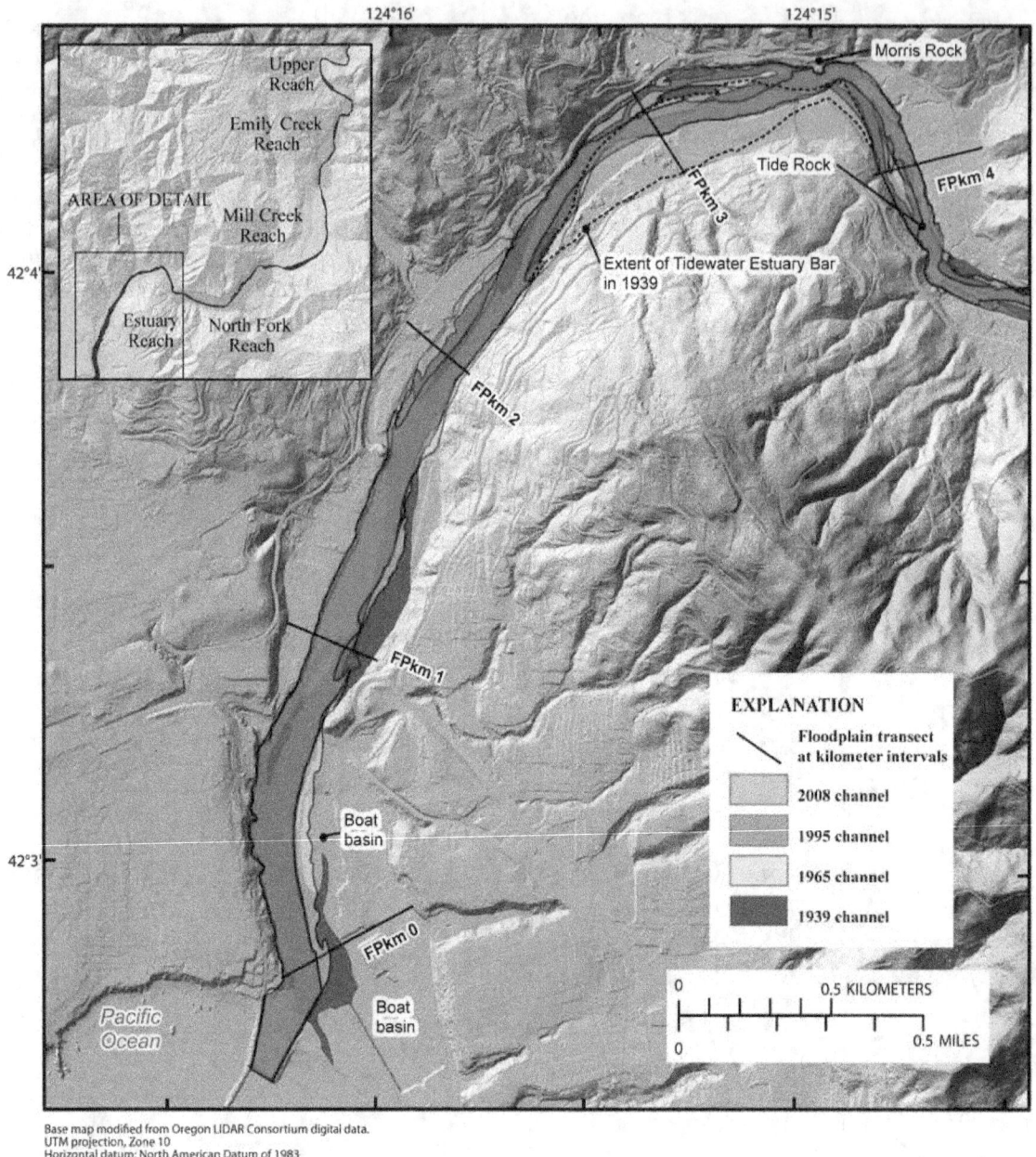

Figure 12. Map showing channel changes between floodplain kilometer 0 and 4.5, encompassing the Estuary Reach, Chetco River, Oregon, 1939–2008. FPkm, floodplain kilometer.

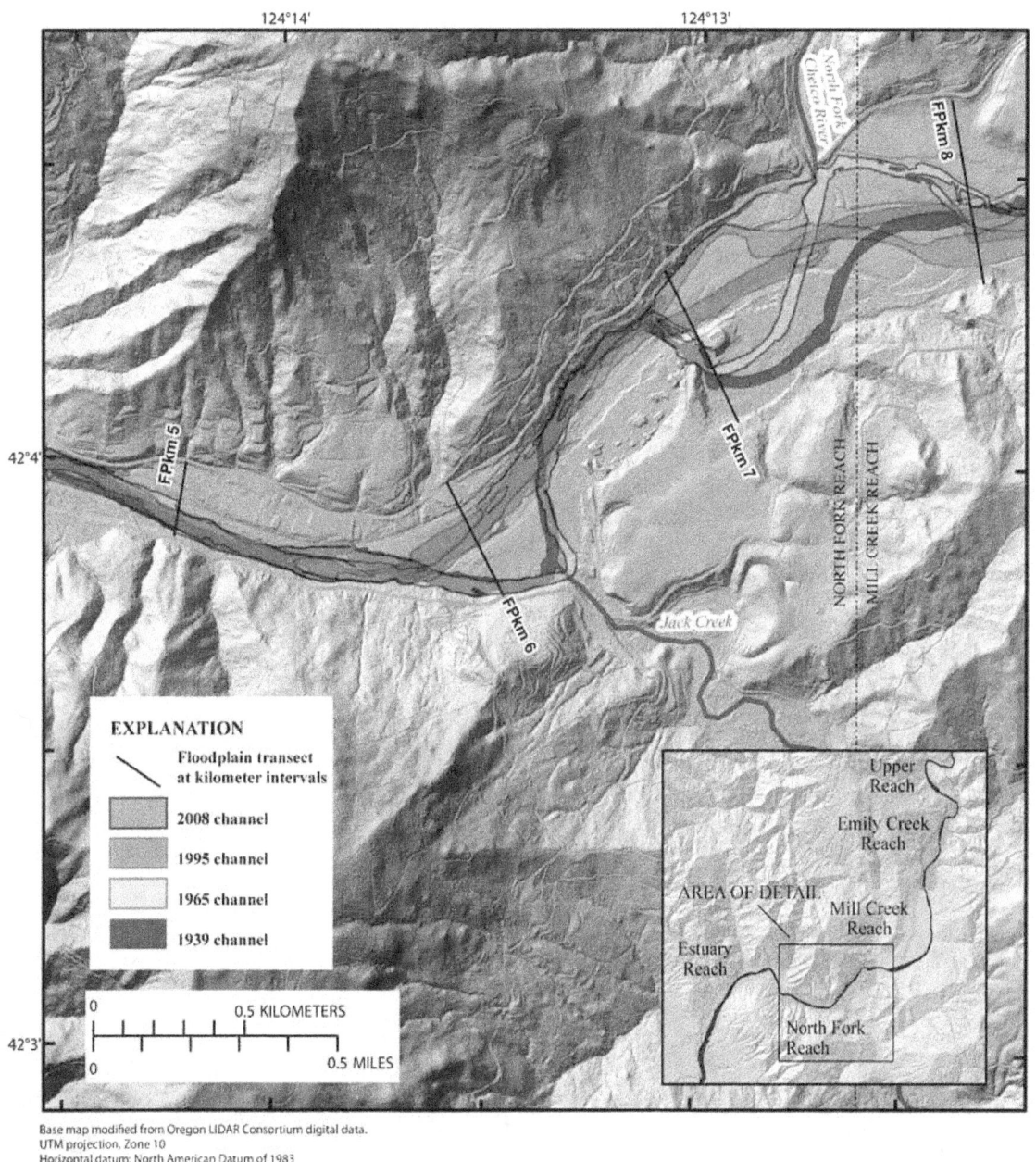

Figure 13. Map showing channel changes between floodplain kilometer 4.5 and 8.4 encompassing the North Fork Reach, Chetco River, Oregon, 1939–2008. FPkm, floodplain kilometer.

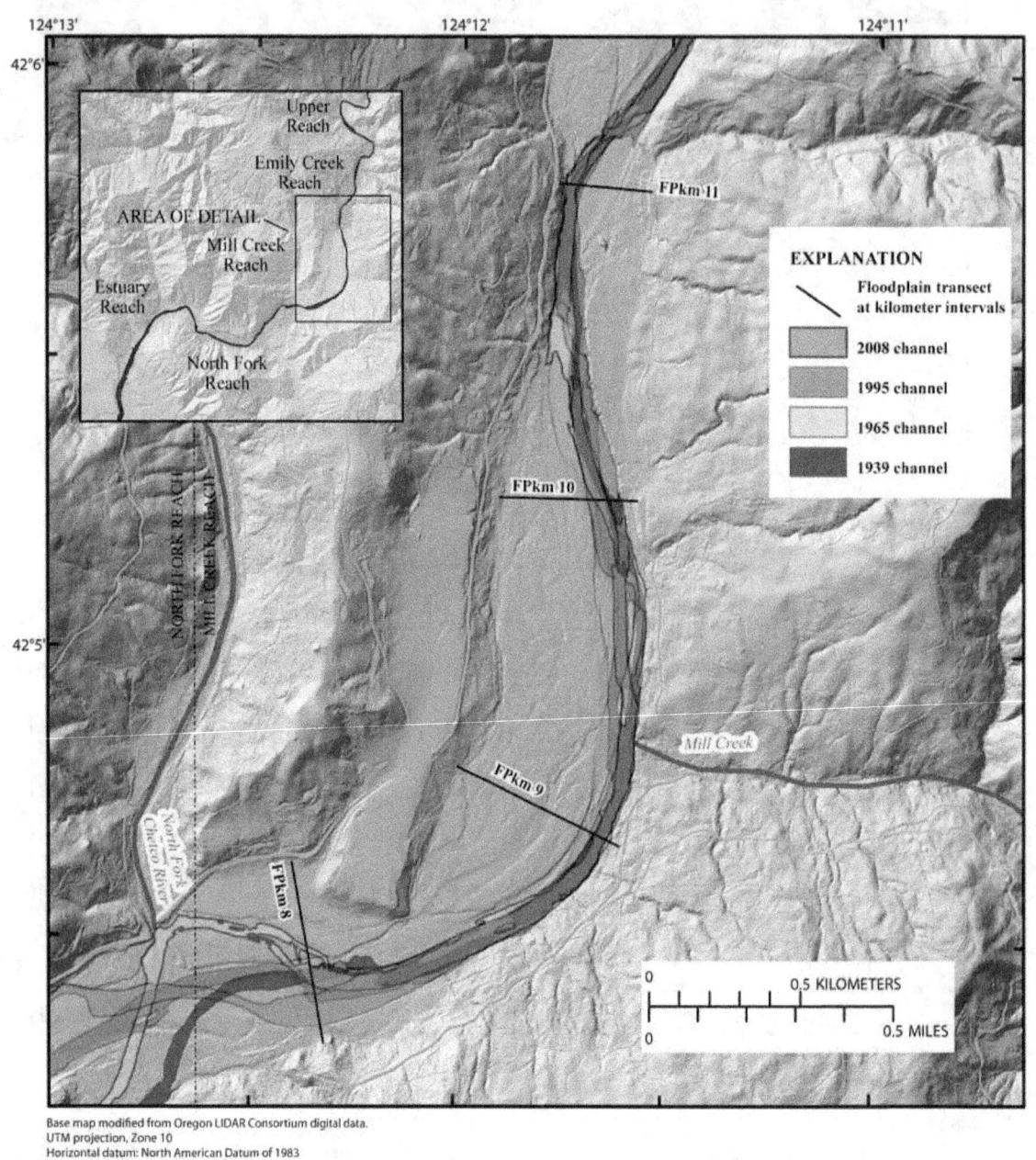

Figure 14. Map showing channel changes between floodplain kilometer 7.5 and 11.5 encompassing the Mill Creek Reach, Chetco River, Oregon, 1939–2008. FPkm, floodplain kilometer.

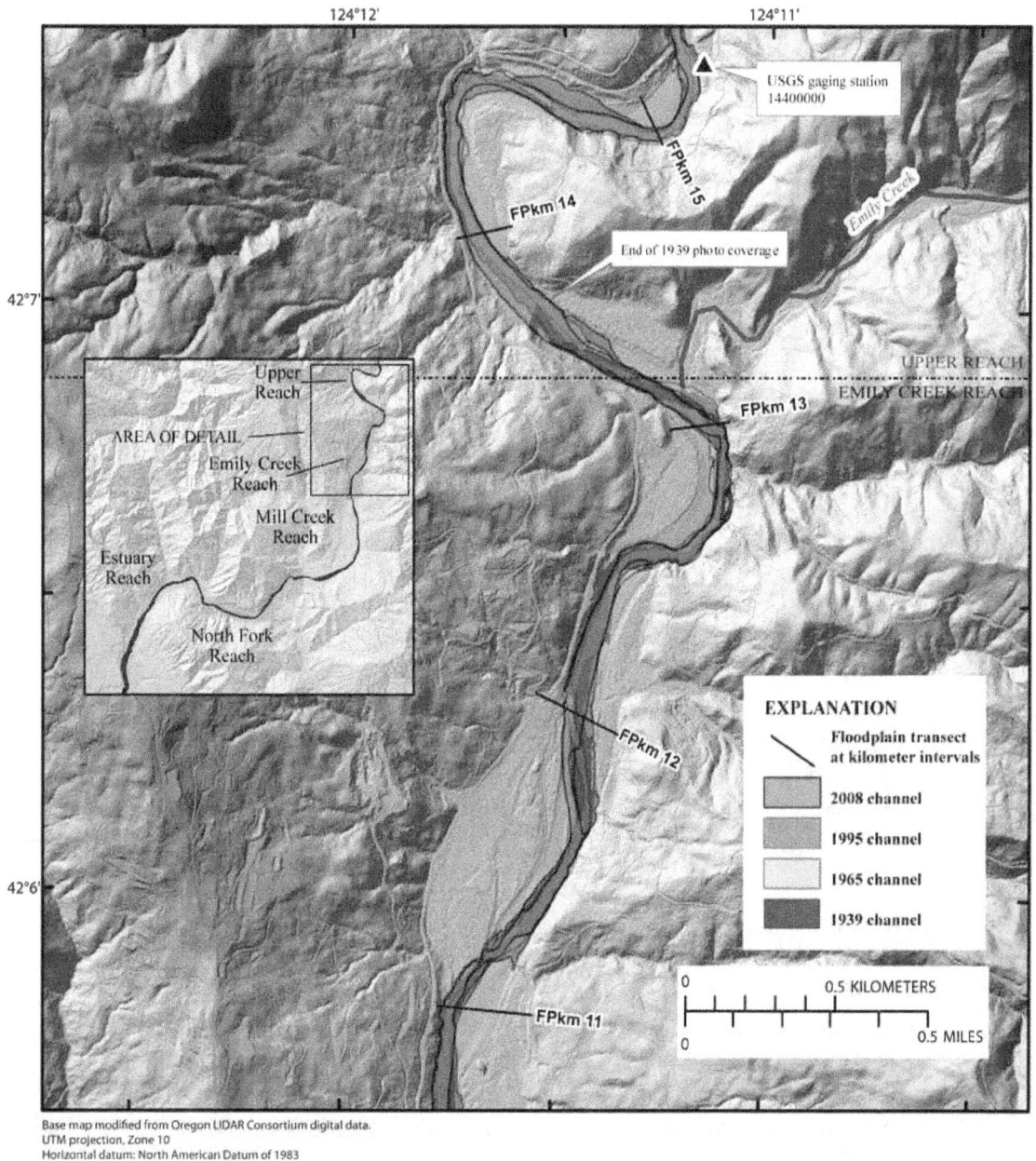

Figure 15. Map showing channel changes between floodplain kilometer 10.6 and floodplain kilometer 15.2 of the Chetco River, Oregon, along the Upper and Emily Creek Reaches, 1939–2008. 1939 coverage extends only to floodplain kilometer 13.7. FPkm, floodplain kilometer.

Inspection of the individual photography sets show that the changes along the North Fork Reach took place in several steps. During 1943–1962, channel migration at rates of up to 14 m/yr between photography sets created a large meander bend near the confluence of the North Fork Chetco River (FPkm 7.5). During winter 1969–70, a large bend near the confluence of Jack Creek[1] (FPkm 6) was cut off and abandoned (probably during the January 1970 flood of nearly 1,900 m^3/s. Between 1969 and 1976, two similar avulsions resulted in abandonment of the North Fork bend (FPkm 7.5) and a smaller bend near FPkm 6[2]. It is likely that the two avulsions at FPkm 6 and 7.5 were during the 1970–72 period of large floods with peak discharges of 1,300–1,900 m^3/s (fig. 2). These avulsions in the late 1960s and early 1970s account for the major decrease in sinuosity for the North Fork Reach between 1965 and 1995 (fig. 9). Partly as a consequence of these channel changes, bank revetment has been placed along these channel margins in the North Fork Reach, so that revetment and bedrock now border 47 percent of the reach in contrast to more than 75 percent of the North Fork Reach being historically bordered by erodible alluvial floodplain materials (fig. 11). In recent decades, the lower Mill Creek Reach and North Fork Reach have been much less dynamic than for the period 1939–1965, shifting laterally at rates less than 6 m/yr and with no significant avulsions (figs. 13 and 14).

Along the Estuary Reach, the overall style of planform change from 1939 to 2008 has been lateral shifting of the channel between the confining valley walls, in conjunction with substantial loss of net bar area (figs. 9, 10, and 12). For example, near FPkm 3, channel maps from 1939 to 1965 show the low flow channel against bedrock along right bank, and a large (150,000 m^2) gravel bar (known locally as "Tidewater Estuary Bar") along the left bank. Between 1965 and 1989,[3] the channel shifted south to erode much of this bar (fig. 12). Additionally, higher elevation areas of Tidewater Estuary Bar, which appear bare and recently active in the photographs from 1939 to 1965, were protected by revetment and developed for residential and commercial use by 1989. The cumulative result of these types of changes is that bar area for the Estuary Reach has decreased 36 percent between 1939 and 2008, although bar area has recently increased between 2005 and 2008 (figs. 9 and 10). Development along the Estuary Reach has resulted in extensive bank stabilization; 41 percent of the channel margin is now bordered by revetment (fig. 11).

Significant changes to the mouth of the Chetco River are the result of 20th century development and navigational improvements that began in the 1950s. The aerial photography from 1939 and 1943 depict the mouth of the Chetco River as approximately 200 m wide, with extensive sand bars and tidal lagoon. By 1962, a pair of jetties restricted channel width and closed off the former lagoon. By 1995, continued bank protection, jetty extension and filling of former lagoon areas resulted in an overall straightening and narrowing of the channel so that channel width at the mouth presently ranges from 100 to 120 m; about half the width shown on the earliest maps and photos (fig. 13).

Channel change along the middle and upper reaches of the study area has been much less than for the lower Mill Creek, North Fork and Estuary Reaches. Within the Emily Creek and Upper Reaches, as well as the upper part of the Mill Creek Reach, the channel crosses back and forth between the valley walls, with intervening channel-flanking gravel bars. The general pattern and positions have remained generally stable, with the most stable locations being where the channel abuts the bedrock valley walls

---

[1] Timing of avulsion is based on inspection of un-rectified aerial photographs provided by the Bureau of Land Management.
[2] Timing of these avulsions is based on inspection of photographs from 1969 provided by the Bureau of Land Management and aerial photography from 1976 used as base map in the Flood Hazard study for the Chetco River (Soil Conservation Service, 1979).
[3] Timing of channel change is based on aerial photographs from 1965 (this study) and unrectified aerial photography provided by the Bureau of Land Management.

(figs. 14 and 15). In isolated locations, the river has migrated laterally at rates up to 6 m/yr where crossing from valley side to side. Where the valley bottom widens towards the lower portion of the Mill Creek Reach (FPkm 7.5-8.5), the channel has been more active, particularly in the period from 1943 to 1962 when rapid migration resulted in the formation of a large meander bend near the North Fork confluence (fig. 14).

Results of Land Cover Mapping

The land cover and vegetation mapping shows that the dominant land cover for the geomorphic floodplain is *Mature Trees*, covering about 30 percent of the floodplain in 2005 and primarily consisting of floodplain forests outside of the active channel (fig. 16). In total, *Water* occupies about 20 percent of the floodplain at low flow. *Developed* area accounts for about 30 percent of the floodplain area along the Estuary Reach in 2005. The *Mature Trees* category systematically decreases as a percentage of floodplain area downstream, as does *Water* except for the North Fork and Estuary Reaches. *Developed* area is only significant in the North Fork and Estuary Reaches, and primarily for the 1962 and more recent photographs. The most dynamic classes are the *Bare*, and the *Sparse, Herbaceous*, and *Woody Shrub* vegetation categories, which cover the greatest relative area in the Mill Creek and North Fork Reaches. These cover-type vegetation classes are chiefly associated with gravel bars subject to colonizing vegetation. No obvious trends are evident for these classes except that the combined area of *Water, Bare*, and *Sparse* vegetation was greatest for all four reaches in 1965, mostly at the expense of *Woody Shrub* and *Mature Trees* categories, likely indicating floodplain erosion and vegetation removal by the flood in 1964.

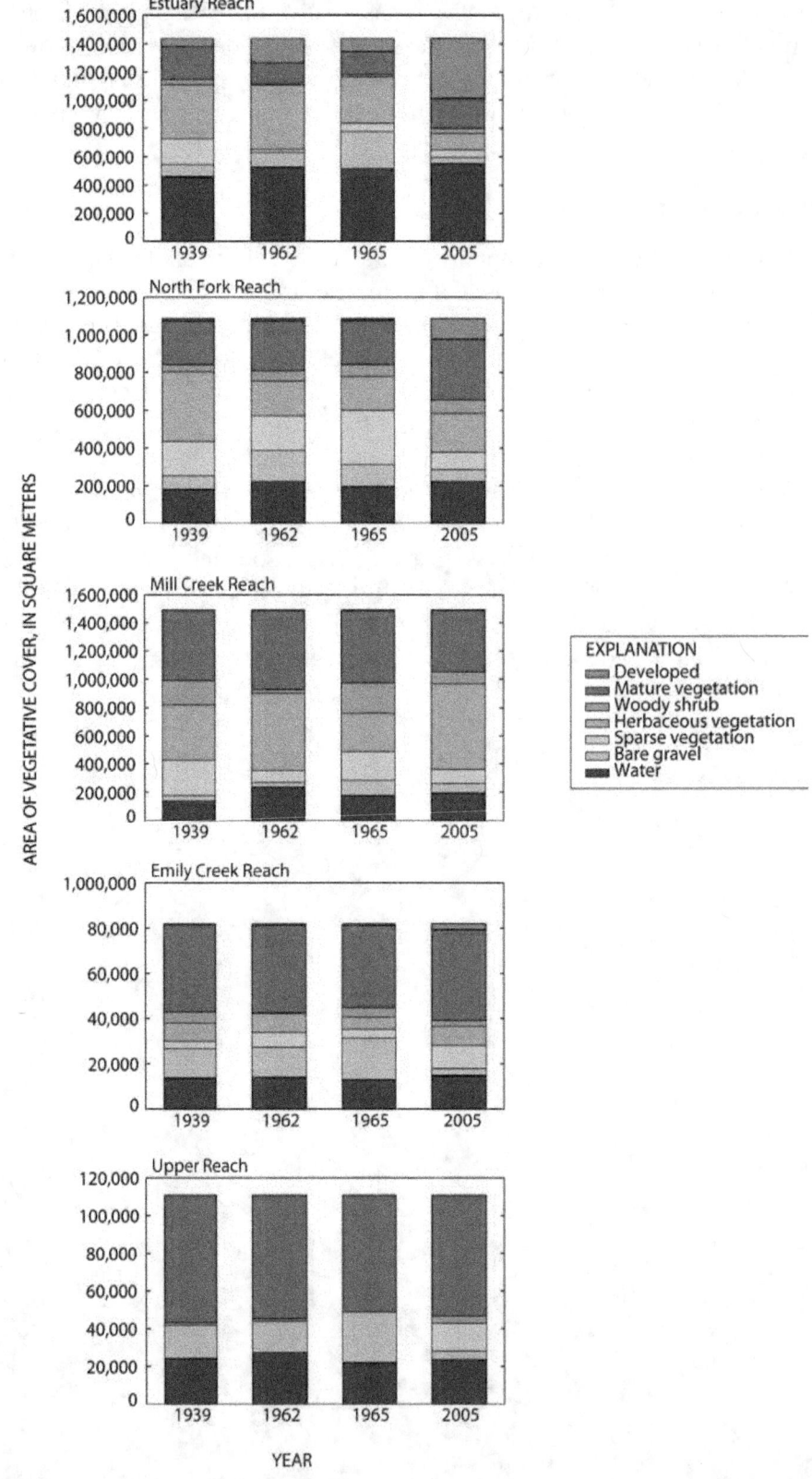

Figure 16. Graphs showing changes in floodplain landcover by analysis reach, Chetco River, Oregon, 1939–2005. Upper Reach data includes only the 0.5 km length of floodplain covered by the aerial photographs from 1939.

Vertical Changes in Channel Morphology and Bathymetry

Although lateral channel changes may have significant resource, habitat, and hazard consequences, changes in the vertical position of the bed are more indicative of riverwide changes in the balance between sediment input and export (Schmidt and Wilcock, 2008). Vertical changes are also more difficult to detect without systematic surveys of the channel. For this study we have compared two previous lengthy surveys—a U.S. Army Corps of Engineers navigational survey in 1939 for the Estuary Reach between FPkm 0 and 4.5, and a 1977 survey for a Soil Conservation Service (1979) flood study of the upstream reaches between FPkm 4 and 15—with the LIDAR topography acquired in 2008 and our own surveys during summer 2008 made as part of this study. Additional local bed elevation information comes from repeat surveys of isolated cross sections in the fluvial reaches as well as the detailed information on channel bed changes from streamflow measurements at the USGS gaging station at FPkm 15.24.

Survey data used in study

Of several early surveys near the mouth of the Chetco River (table 3), the most useful survey for characterizing channel morphology along the Estuary Reach is the navigational survey of 1939 (U.S. Army Corps of Engineers, 1939), in which closely spaced soundings and elevations in feet relative to Mean Lower Low Water (MLLW) are provided for FPkm 0 to 4.5. Details of digitizing, georeferencing, and datum conversion are included in the metadata for the accompanying GIS maps (U.S. Geological Survey, 2009), but in summary, this survey included more than 1,000 points over the lowermost 4.5 km of channel. The survey from 1939 was compared to a USGS bathymetric survey in September and October 2008 between FPkm 0 and 3. This boat-based survey used a depth-sounding transducer mounted directly below a real-time kinematic (RTK) global positioning system (GPS) receiver. As the survey boat traversed the estuary at transects spaced at 30 to 50 m intervals, the depth-sounder recorded water depth while the GPS recorded the boat position and GPS ellipsoid height for a total of nearly 200,000 points (complete metadata and GIS layers available in U.S. Geological Survey, 2009).

The bathymetric data of 1939 and 2008 for the Chetco River estuary were interpolated to three-dimensional surfaces using a modified version of the procedure of Merwade and others (2005), which entails transforming the data into a channel oriented coordinate system, interpolating a continuous surface using anisotropic kriging, and reprojecting the surface back to the project coordinate system of UTM NAD83 (fig. 17). Once the bathymetric surfaces were created, longitudinal profiles of the channel thalweg from each time period were extracted and plotted against river kilometers for 2008.

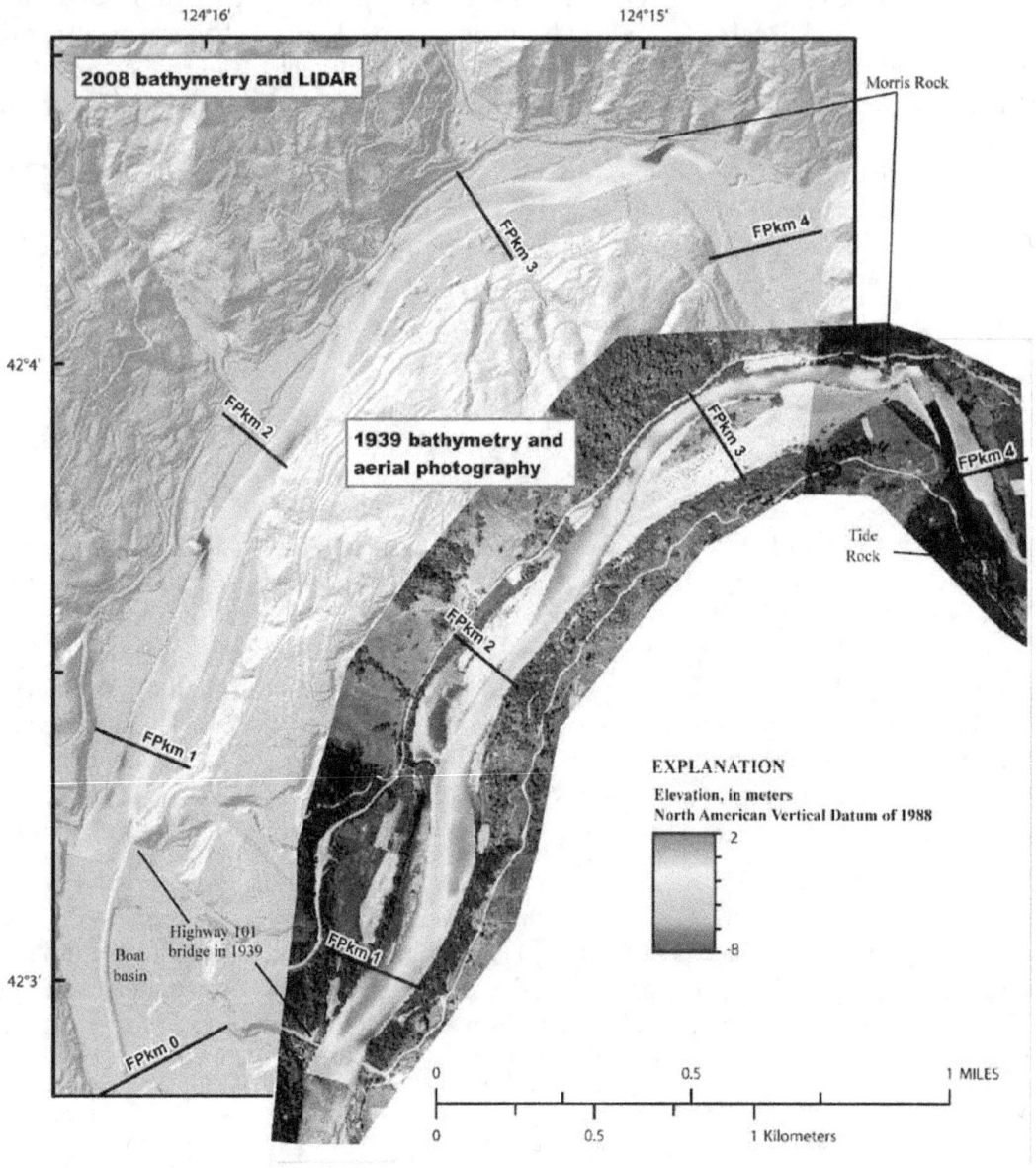

Figure 17. Map showing bathymetry for 1939 and 2008 between floodplain kilometer 0.6 and 3.7, Chetco River, Oregon. Bathymetry from 1939 derived from U.S. Army Corps of Engineers (1939); bathymetry for 2008 from this study. Map and survey processing described in metadata for the supporting GIS files is, available from the USGS (U.S. Geological Survey, 2009, at http://or.water.usgs.gov/chetco/.)

To determine vertical channel changes along the upstream fluvial reaches of the study area between FPkm 4 and 15, longitudinal profiles and cross sections were compiled from a 1977 survey and compared to 2008 elevation data and surveys. In 1977, 42 cross sections across the entire valley bottom between FPkm 0 and 15.5 were surveyed as part of a flood hazard study by the Soil Conservation Service (1979). The location of each survey transect was depicted on orthophotographs from 1976, and cross-section data shown by plots of distance (in feet from an arbitrary point) against elevation (in feet referenced to NGVD 29 datum). From this information, cross section locations and data were digitized by visually plotting survey transects shown in the orthophotos from 1976 onto the orthophotos from 2005. The elevations for 1977 were shifted from NGVD 29 datum to the NAVD 88 datum using the CorpsCon conversion routine (*http://crunch.tec.army.mil/software/corpscon/corpscon.html*, accessed January, 13, 2009) and by comparing elevations of benchmarks surveyed in 1977 and 2008 throughout the study area.

We approximately matched nine of these cross sections from 1977 by (1) using October 2008 RTK GPS and depth-sounder surveys of the active channel at the estimated locations of the cross sections from 1977, (2) merging these October 2008 channel surveys with the LIDAR from May–June 2008 to extend the surveys for 2008 across the valley bottom, and (3), where required, shifting the cross section data from 1977 laterally so that obvious and stable topographic features such as road beds and steep banks were aligned with those on the cross sections for 2008. Such adjustments were necessary in a few cases as a consequence of not being able to precisely locate the cross section locations for 1977. The survey in 2008 also produced a nearly complete longitudinal profile of the channel thalweg from FPkm 4 to 15 (fig. 4), which can be compared to the minimum elevation for each of the 42 cross sections surveyed in 1977. These surveys were supplemented by ancillary survey data for 1980–82 reported by Klingeman (1993; fig. 18).

The final source of vertical change information is from analysis of the history of stage-discharge rating curves at the USGS streamflow measurement station at FPkm 15.2. Following the approach of Klingeman (1973) and Smelser and Schmidt (1998), we conducted a specific gage analysis for the available record from October 1, 1969, to May 1, 2009. The specific gage analysis allows detection of changes in streambed elevation by assessing changes in water elevation (stage) through time for a set of discharge values. At USGS streamflow-gaging stations, discharge is related to stage by a stage-discharge rating curve, which is based on multiple simultaneous measurements of stage and discharge. If channel conditions change substantially (as evidenced by consistent offsets of newer measurements from established rating curves), or if a station is moved, a new rating curve will be developed. The specific gage analysis evaluates trends in bed elevation as indicated by the sequence of rating curves. For situations where channel width and roughness remain stable, the sequence of stages for a given discharge directly relates to changes in bed elevation. For the Chetco River, the analysis is straightforward because there have been no relocations or datum shifts for the station, although the record is shorter than for many USGS streamflow measurement stations and 3 of the 39 ratings were unavailable.

Uncertainty and Limitations Associated with the Repeat Survey Data

The total uncertainty regarding the resulting bathymetric surfaces created from the survey data of 1939 and 2008 is a function of the original data and the processing involved with creating digital maps and interpolated surfaces of the bathymetries. Although the accuracy of the original map from 1939 is unknown, the process by which the original map was registered, rectified, and digitized may have introduced uncertainty on the order of ± 20 m for the horizontal positioning of points, but in most locations is substantially less. The interpolation procedure introduces additional error and uncertainty, thus the total accuracy of the bathymetry for 1939 is estimated to be ±20 m for horizontal and 1 m in the vertical dimension as determined from distribution of differences between the digitized survey points and the gridded elevation data. Each of the points from the bathymetric survey in 2008 has a horizontal accuracy of ±0.015 m and a vertical accuracy of approximately ±0.05 m. The interpolated bathymetric surface in 2008 is generally within ±0.3 m of the original survey elevations.

The survey in 1977 by the Soil Conservation Service (1979) was in support of a flood hazard study and preparation of flood hazard maps. The survey is described (Soil Conservation Service, 1979, p. E-1) as a "third order field survey" using USGS base elevations. For such surveys, elevation tolerances (RMSE) are typically less than 0.15 m (American Society of Civil Engineers, 1999, p. 6). The conversion of the original sea level (NGVD 29) datum to NAVD 88 is straightforward and the converted data match resurveys in 2008 of benchmarks used in the 1977 to within 0.05 m. Therefore, the primary source of uncertainty regarding the survey in 1977 is its horizontal positioning. The only available information for the precise location of the measurements for 1977 is the 1:4,800 photomosaic maps in the Soil Conservation Service (1979) report. On the basis of these maps, the cross section locations for 1977 were digitized onto the photomosaic for 2005 used for this analysis by reference to stable features visible on both photography sets. We judge the uncertainty associated with the horizontal placement of the cross sections from 1977 on the maps for 2005 to be everywhere less than 150 m. Such an offset in conjunction with the 0.001 average slope of the study reach would introduce vertical errors of less than 0.15 m attributable to uncertainty in horizontal cross section position for thalweg and water-surface elevations (assuming uniform slope and depth). The accuracy of the cross-section data surveyed in 2008 as a part of this study is approximately ±0.015 m, whereas vertical accuracy is approximately ±0.05 m. Discrepancies between the cross-section alignments in 1977 and 2008 cause some cross sections of 1977 to portray slightly different areas of the bar and floodplain than are depicted in the matching cross section of 2008; therefore, the cross sections are best viewed in terms of overall trends, especially for thalweg elevations, as differences in bank geometry do not necessarily indicate channel shifting.

Results of Repeat Surveys

Comparison of bathymetric surfaces within the Estuary Reach from 1939 and 2008 shows that the bed of the Chetco River was generally lower in 2008 than in 1939 (fig. 17). A difference calculation for the bathymetric surfaces for 1939 and 2008 between FPkm 0.5 and 3.5, corresponding to the reach between the Highway 101 Bridge to Morris Rock, indicates a net loss of 150,000 m^3 of channel substrate between 1939 and 2008. This corresponds to an average lowering of the entire channel bottom by about 0.5 m. Locally, however, there are three primary locations where channel shifting has resulted in much greater magnitudes of incision and aggradation (fig. 17). Near FPkm 3, the channel historically flowed against the right bank with bottom elevations of approximately 0.5 m (NAVD 88). By 2008, the channel had shifted towards the left bank and had deepened by 0.2 to 2.0 m, with the bed elevations in 2008 ranging from 0.3 to -1.5 m (NAVD 88). Near FPkm 1.7 a large alcove in 1939 extended nearly 0.5 km from the right bank. By 2008, this alcove had aggraded by approximately 1 m, and the main arm of the alcove is presently filled with sediments and partially vegetated. Near FPkm 1.0 and just upstream of the Hwy 101 Bridge, the channel in 1939 flowed against the left valley wall, carving a deep channel with bed elevations ranging from –1.5 to –4 m (NAVD 88). By 2008, the channel had shifted to the right bank, and the thalweg from 1939 is presently an alcove with bed elevations of about –0.6 m. The thalweg of 2008 in this area is shallower (bed elevations of –1.5 to –2.5 m NAVD 88) and lacks the deep pool depicted in the survey from 1939.

For the short reach between FPkm 1.5 and 4.3, where all three surveys overlap, the longitudinal profiles from 1939, 1977, and 2008 indicate net lowering of the channel thalweg between 1939 and 2008 (fig. 18A). The magnitude of lowering is as great as 2 m, with the reach above FPkm 2 showing the most consistent bed lowering. The resolution of the survey in 1977 is not sufficient to clearly indicate whether the majority of the channel incision in the estuary was before or after 1977, but the survey in 1977 does show that the channel had at least locally aggraded by nearly 1 m near the Highway 101 bridge at FPkm 0.85 between 1939 and 1977 before incising back to its elevation of 1939 by 2008.

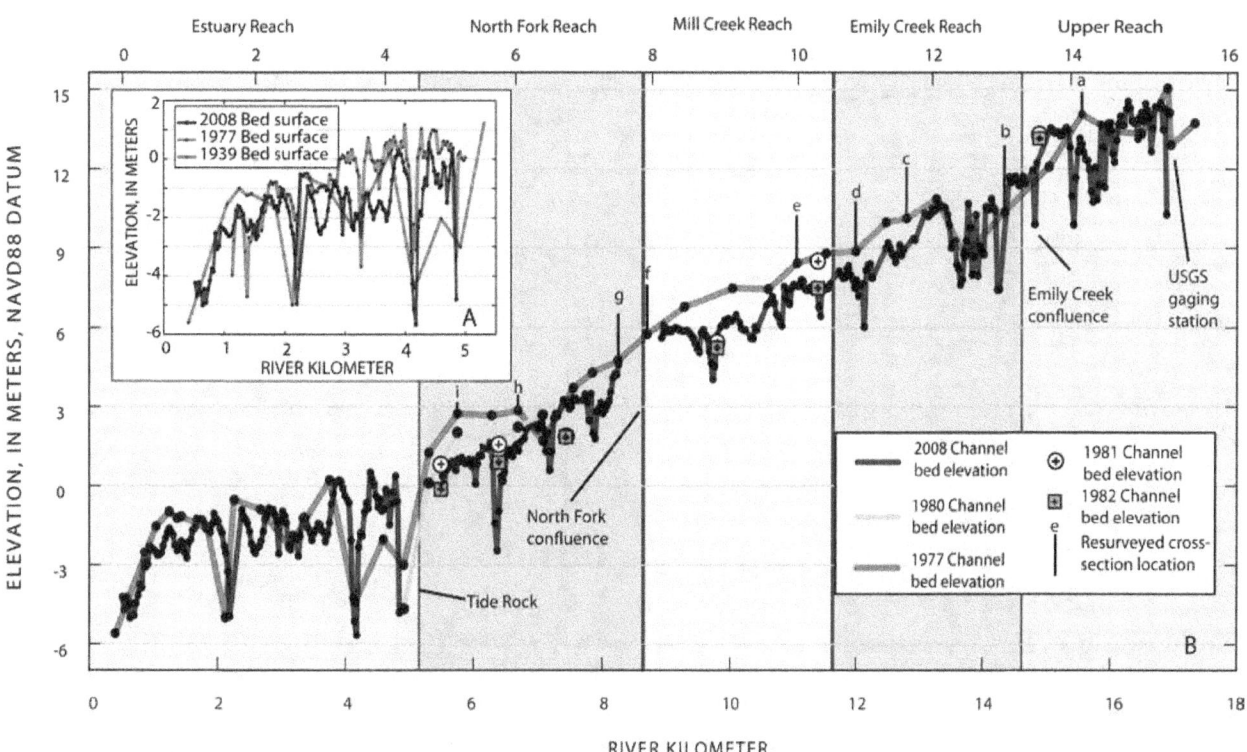

Figure 18. Graph showing channel thalweg profiles below river kilometer 18, Chetco River, Oregon. A. Channel thalweg profiles for Estuary Reach from bathymetric survey of 1939 (U.S. Army Corps of Engineers, 1939), cross sections from 1977 flood study survey (Soil Conservation Service, 1979), and USGS bathymetric survey in 2008. B. Channel thalweg profiles from bathymetric survey in 1939 (U.S. Army Corps of Engineers, 1939), flood study survey in 1977 (Soil Conservation Service, 1979), and USGS channel survey in 2008. Thalweg elevations for surveys in 1980–82 are from Oregon Department of State Lands surveys, as reported by Klingeman (1993).

Upstream of the Estuary Reach and the extent of the bathymetric surveys, comparison of longitudinal profiles derived from surveys in 1977 and 2008 shows mainly bed lowering, especially between FPkm 4.5 and 6 in the North Fork Reach and between FPkm 8 and 12 in the Mill Creek and Emily Creek Reaches. In these locations, the channel is consistently 1–2 m lower in 2008 than it was in 1977 (fig. 18B). This apparent lowering exceeds plausible uncertainties owing to survey accuracy. For the Upper Reach upstream of FPkm 12, net changes in bed elevation between the surveys in 1977 and 2008 have been small. In the Estuary Reach, the difference between the surveys in 1977 and 2008 indicate possible thalweg aggradation for the kilometer downstream of Tide Rock, but here the resolution of the survey in 1977 is poor in comparison to the bathymetric surveys (fig. 18A) which show net incision of about 1 m between 1939 and 2008.

Sparser measurements from 1980, 1981, and 1982, which were surveyed in relation to the survey in 1977 (Klingeman, 1993), indicate that a substantial portion of the channel lowering in the Estuary, North Fork, and Mill Creek reaches was before 1982 at some locations (fig. 18A). Examination of the repeat surveys of the cross sections surveyed in 1977 and 2008 (fig. 19) indicate that channel lowering between FPkm 4 and FPkm 12 was independent of the rest of the active channel, as bar elevations appear similar in 1977 and 2008 (particularly for cross sections e, f, and g in fig. 19).

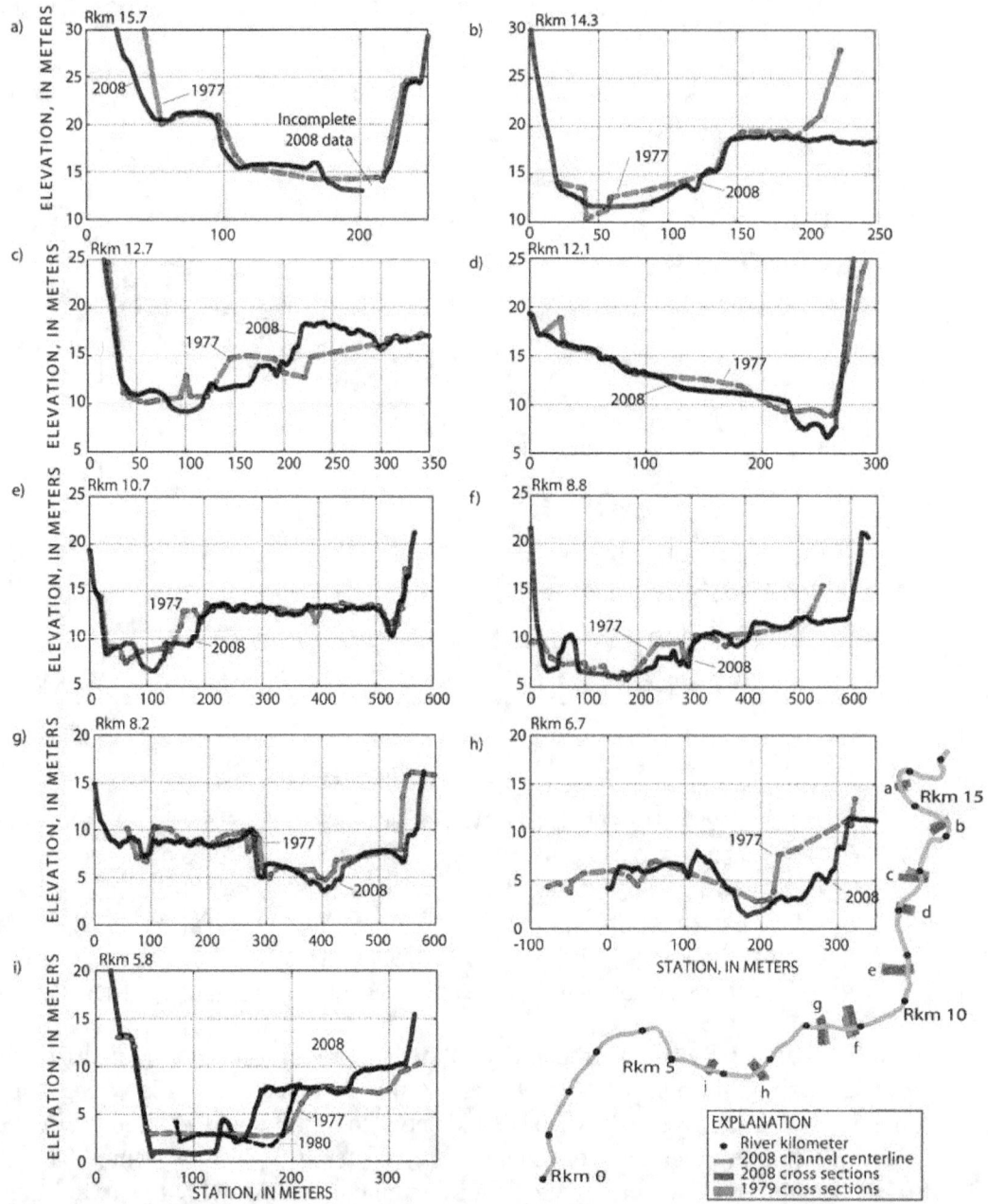

Figure 19. Graph showing comparison cross-sections from the flood study survey in 1977, digitized from Soil Conservation Service (1979) and approximately relocated during the USGS resurveys in September 2008, Chetco River, Oregon. Imperfect relocation results in discrepancies for some sections, but all are judged to be within 150 m of original location. Cross section locations also shown on figure 18B profile plots.

Information collected during the course of flow measurements at the USGS gaging station at FPkm 15.24 provides another source of quantitative information on channel change (fig. 20). The specific gage analysis (fig. 20A) encompasses 39 separate ratings over nearly 30 years. The large number of ratings is in itself indicative of frequent changes in local geometry and substantial bed-material transport. For comparison, the South Umpqua River near Brockway has had only 11 ratings since 1942 (O'Connor and others, 2009). The ratings for the lower discharges are sensitive to scour and fill of low-flow pools and riffles near the measurement section and consequently show more variation. For example, the rating for the 5.5 m^3/s flow shows an overall trend of bed lowering after a period of slightly higher stages in the late 1970s, consistent with the ratings for all discharges, but with a total variation of 1.2 m. The ratings for the larger flows reflect more general reach scale channel and floodplain conditions, including the volume of gravel in the bar flanking the left margin of the channel (fig. 20B), and indicate an overall lowering of flow-stage elevations since 1970, although with smaller magnitudes of change. But within the overall lowering trend, the high-flow ratings show evidence of aggradation and narrowing in the late 1970s as well in 1997, after the 2,169 m^3/s peak discharge in 1996. For all flow ratings, however, the overall trend has been a net decline of flow stage associated with specific discharges, ranging from 0.86 m for the low flows to 0.28 m for the higher analyzed discharges. The series of ratings, especially for the larger discharges, also indicate aggradation of approximately 0.2–0.3 m culminating between 1976 and 1978, followed by nearly continuous decline until an episode of aggradation in the late 1990s, interrupted by aggradation and narrowing after the 1996 flood. Since 2000, all ratings have declined between 0.2 and 0.4 m (fig. 20A).

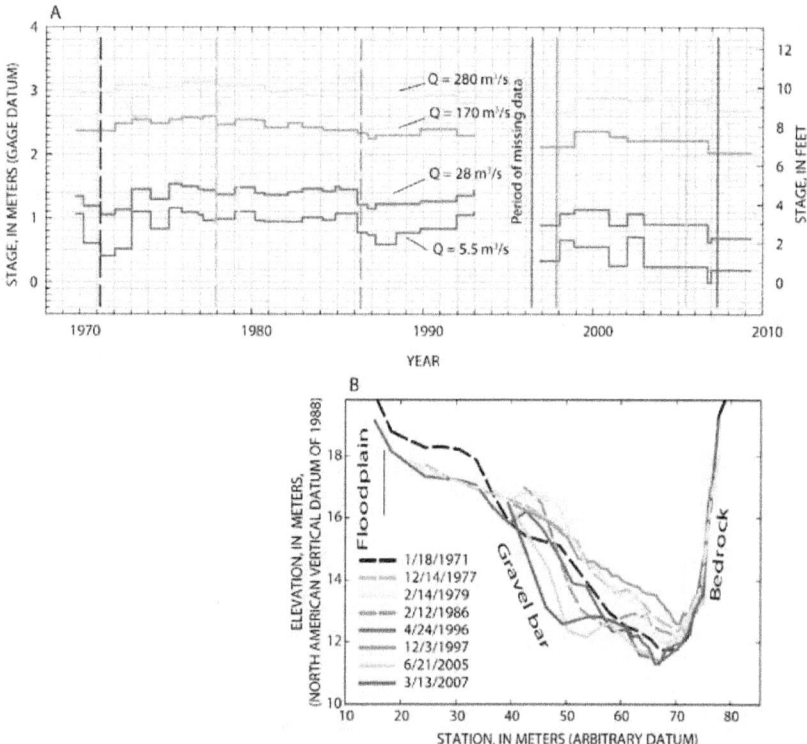

Figure 20. Graph showing specific gage analysis and flow-measurement cross sections for the USGS streamflow gage Chetco River near Brookings, OR (14400000). A. Specific gage analysis following approach of Klingeman (1973) and encompassing 39 ratings used between 1970 and 2008. Rating curves available at the Oregon Water Science Center in Portland, Oregon. Data for ratings 28–30 not available. B. Selected cross sections extracted from flow measurements at station cableway. Cross sections extend to flow edge for each measurement.

Summary and Discussion of Historical Channel Change

The main observation from the planview mapping is a large decrease in bar (and bare gravel) area along the entire study area between 1939 and 2008. Historical changes in bar area, channel width, and sinuosity have been greatest near the confluence of the North Fork Chetco River, within the Mill Creek and North Fork Reaches, and downstream through the Estuary Reach. The largest changes were between 1965 and 1995, with the periods before and after showing little change or perhaps even opposite trends. The repeat surveys and specific gage analysis indicate that the overall historical vertical change has been bed lowering. Repeat surveys in the estuary show that the channel in 2008 was on average about 0.5 m lower than the channel was in 1939. Similarly, stretches of the Emily Creek, Mill Creek, and North Fork Reaches appear to have channel thalweg elevations up to 2 m lower in 2008 than were measured in the surveys of 1977, with much of the lowering perhaps occurring between 1977 and 1981. The specific gage analysis at FPkm 15.2 (Upper Reach) indicates episodes of aggradation in the late 1970s and late 1990s, but overall a long-term trend of bed lowering.

Many factors are likely responsible for these changes, including (1) direct physical alteration of the river corridor by bank stabilization and development, (2) bars evolving to floodplain by accumulation of overbank sediment and vegetation colonization, (3) changes in the volume of bed-material sediment brought into the study reach from upstream and tributary sources, either because of flow history or drainage basin conditions, (4) changes in the volume of sediment transported out study area by fluvial processes or by dredging and gravel extraction, and (5) floods, which are commonly a catalyst for change.

For the Estuary Reach, the channel and floodplain have been extensively modified by dredging, jetty construction and development between FPkm 0 and 2. Upstream within this reach, commercial aggregate removal may be a factor in decreased bar areas, but bank protection, fill, and development has also reduced bar area.

For the North Fork and Mill Creek Reaches, the planview changes reflect the complicated interplay between the normal pattern of meander growth followed by cutoffs in wandering and sediment-rich rivers (Church, 1983; O'Connor and others, 2003), episodic tributary sediment input from the North Fork Chetco River and possibly Jack Creek, large mainstem floods triggering episodes of channel change, and the direct channel disturbance and indirect consequences of the long history of substantial gravel extraction in this reach. The channel lowering, decreased recent rates of channel migration, diminished bar area, and lesser amounts of bare gravel and sparse vegetation are all mutually consistent changes indicative of transformation from sediment surplus to bed material deficit. Such transformations would promote the conversion of bars to floodplain surfaces as illustrated in figure 21.

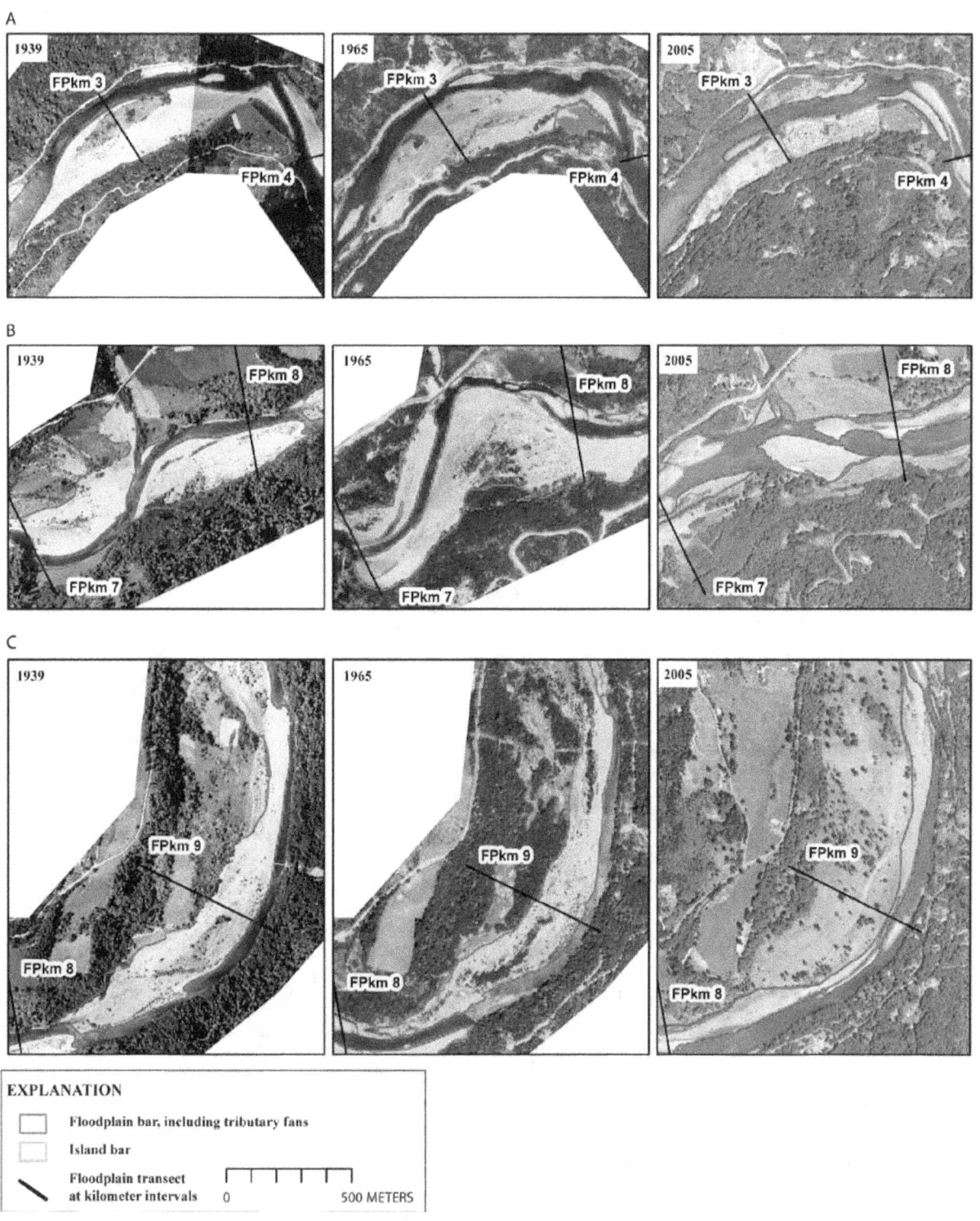

Figure 21. Photographs showing examples of bar evolution to floodplain and developed areas between 1939 and 2005, Chetco River, Oregon. FPkm, Floodplain kilometer. A. Gravel bar near floodplain kilometer 3 (Estuary Reach) evolving to developed area. B. Dynamic bars between floodplain kilometer 7 and 9 (North Fork and Mill Creek Reaches). C. Example of vegetation colonization on upper bar surface near floodplain kilometer 9 (Mill Creek Reach).

The Upper and Emily Creek Reaches have had more stable planforms, reflecting the strong control imposed by the closer valley walls. Although bar elevations were similar in 1977 and 2008, the Emily Creek Reach shows evidence of decreased bar area (fig. 9) and local bed lowering (fig. 18) during between 1939 and 2008. Similarly, the specific gage analysis shows general trends of bed lowering and bar erosion near the gage location in the Upper Reach since the late 1970s (fig. 20). The changes in these two reaches could either be the result of reduced supply from upstream relative to transport capacity or incision propagating from downstream areas where there has historically been substantial gravel extraction.

An important factor in the evolution of channel and floodplain of the lower Chetco River is the history of large flows, since they are probably responsible for bringing in large volumes of sediment and triggering channel change. The largest gaged flow was 2,155 m^3/s on November 19, 1996, but the December 22, 1964, flood with estimated discharge of 2,420 m^3/s (*http://wdr.water.usgs.gov/wy2008/pdfs/14400000.2008.pdf*), was of exceptional duration, and is the largest known flood for the river (Soil Conservation Service, 1979). Anecdotal accounts describe substantial sedimentation along the Chetco River as a consequence of the 1964 flood (Maguire, 2001, p. 9), similar to that documented for several northern California drainages along the Pacific coast (Stewart and LaMarche, 1967; Kelsey, 1980; Madej, 1995). The flood of 1964 in particular caused significant and persistent sedimentation in the Klamath Mountains area because of the great volumes of hillslope material eroded and delivered to the channels during the storm and ensuing flood (Hickey, 1969; Waananen and others, 1971; Lisle, 1981; Harden, 1995). For several southern Oregon and northern California coastal drainage basins, the large volumes of sediment transported to the main channels led to periods of aggradation for mainstem rivers, including the nearby Smith River, for as long as 15 years after the flood, followed by periods of channel incision (Lisle, 1981). Some of the changes seen on the lower Chetco River, such as the late 1970s aggradation at the streamflow measurement station and the subsequent channel lowering (and the attendant reduction in bar areas) may be a similar decadal time-scale response to this particularly significant flood.

Bed Material: Characterization, Transport, and Budget

Partly building on the channel mapping, a primary objective of this study was to estimate the volume of bed material entering the lower Chetco River and the distribution of this material as it is transported and deposited within the study reach. Because of the multiple uncertainties and factors in such an analysis, we have adopted multiple measurement and analysis approaches. The overall analysis framework is that of a sediment budget (for example, Reid and Dunne, 1996, 2003), accounting for the various inputs and outputs of bed material affecting the 16-km-long study reach.

The analysis focused on bed material, the sediment found along the bed of the active channel. For the Chetco River, bed material includes the substrate of the low-flow channel and the flanking gravel bars, and consists chiefly of sand and gravel (clast diameters greater than 0.063 mm and ranging up to 250 mm). These materials are transported through the river corridor primarily as bedload by bouncing, sliding, or rolling along the bed, although some sand (clasts with diameters between 0.063 and 2 mm) may be transported as suspended load, supported higher in the flow by turbulence. The specific factors that require consideration for a bed-material budget are the (1) volume of bed material transported into the reach from upstream, (2) volume of bed material transported directly into the reach by tributaries, (3) volume of bed material leaving the reach by fluvial transport into the Pacific Ocean, (4) volume leaving by other means (dredging, gravel extraction), (5) change in storage within the reach (owing to channel and bar deposition and erosion), and (6) attrition of bed-material clasts by mechanical breakage as they are transported and conversion of some mass of the bed-material load to finer materials. Adding to the challenge posed in considering all these factors is that the fluxes can vary tremendously in space and time (Gomez, 1991).

Two independent approaches were applied to assessing bed-material transport rates and storage throughout the study reach: (1) a transport equation approach in which bed material transport was calculated on the basis of prescribed flow, channel geometry, and sediment conditions, and (2) a mapping based approach in which bed material fluxes were estimated from spatial and temporal changes in the volume of stored sediment along the study reach. Underlying these approaches were basic characterization of the sediment and flow conditions, in addition to the mapping of active channel features as described above.

Bed Material Characterization and Source

There were two objectives in characterizing the bed material. The first was to assess the size distribution of the bed material to support analyses of transport rates and bar-surface armoring. The second was to assess sediment sources and possibly particle attrition rates by evaluating spatial patterns in clast lithology.

Gravel Distribution and Textures

A robust description of the Chetco River bed material is central to understanding overall patterns of sediment storage along the study area. Particle size information also supports sediment flux calculations by bedload-transport equations, as well as inferences of relations between sediment supply, channel morphology, and shear stress (for example, Dietrich and others, 1989; Lisle and others, 2000).

The active gravel bars along the Chetco River study area are expansive (figs. 3, 8, and 21), some extending for lengths greater than 1 km with widths exceeding 0.25 km. The total bar area within the study reach in 2008 is about 0.9 km^2, approximately equal to the total low flow channel area. The mean bar height above the channel thalweg, as determined from the mapping, LIDAR, and longitudinal profile survey, is 3 m.

Sampling

Bed-material textures were characterized by sampling 12 mainstem Chetco River gravel bars along the length of the study reach during September 2008. These data were supplemented by measurements at three tributary channels (table 4). For each of these bars, surface-particle sizes on the bar apex were measured. For three of the Chetco River mainstem bars, additional surface samples at the middle and downstream areas of the bar were measured, and substrate was sampled at the bar apex (table 4). Surface material sampling was by a modified grid technique (Kondolf and others, 2003), measuring grain size for 200 particles at 0.3-m increments along two parallel 30-m tapes. The tapes were spaced 1–2 m apart and were aligned parallel to the long axis of the bar. Clast measurements were by aluminum template (Federal Interagency Sediment Project US SAH-97 Gravelometer).

Table 4. Sediment sampling locations used in the sediment transport study, Chetco River, Oregon

[Samples collected on September 15-19, 2008, using methods of Wolman (1954). Unless otherwise noted, samples were taken at bar apices. Eastings and northings are in meters and refer to the UTM zone 10 projection using the North American Datum of 1983. d_{16}: grain size diameter in millimeters, where 16% of the sample is finer by volume. d_{50}: grain size diameter in millimeters, where 50% of the sample is finer by volume. d_{84}: grain size diameter in millimeters, where 84% of the sample is finer by volume. Location names are informal descriptions of bars based on local landmarks.]

Sample ID	Location	River kilometer	Floodplain kilometer	Easting	Northing	Sample Type	d_{16}	d_{50}	d_{84}
1a	Fitzhugh Bar	17.4	16.3	402185	4664607	surface	7.76	47.19	103.57
						subsurface	2.27	31.08	121.87
1b	Fitzhugh Bar; midbar	17.3	16.0	402067	4664588	surface	10.00	31.72	72.21
1c	Fitzhugh Bar; bar toe	17.0	15.3	401898	4664363	surface	16.73	40.91	74.54
2	Second Bridge Bar	16.7	15.1	401900	4664111	surface	11.52	28.87	57.42
3	Emily Creek Bar	14.5	13.2	401916	4663279	surface, tributary	7.08	22.14	47.00
4	Loeb Park Bar	14.3	13.0	401955	4662994	surface	17.98	37.15	63.07
5	Tamba Bar	12.4	11.3	401353	4661413	surface	10.14	36.33	72.13
6	Mill Creek Bar	10.5	9.5	401281	4659622	surface	20.95	53.26	89.40
7	Freeman Bar	8.6	7.8	400003	4658583	surface	24.26	57.83	101.94
8	North Fork Bar	8.3	7.6	399729	4658916	surface, tributary	16.24	39.22	96.55
9	Jack Creek Bar	6.5	5.9	398949	4657514	surface, tributary	15.38	31.43	70.50
10a	Social Security Bar	6.7	6.1	398602	4657732	surface	14.21	39.72	85.94
						subsurface	1.51	19.01	59.43
10b	Social Security Bar; midbar	6.3	5.6	398249	4657614	surface	4.32	18.89	39.48
10c	Social Security Bar; bar toe	6.0	5.4	397969	4657655	surface	10.10	19.75	37.96
11	Tide Rock Bar	5.1	4.4	397114	4657964	surface	6.15	23.88	58.76

Table 4. Sediment sampling locations used in the sediment transport study, Chetco River, Oregon—continued

[Samples collected on September 15-19, 2008, using methods of Wolman (1954). Unless otherwise noted, samples were taken at bar apices. Eastings and northings are in meters and refer to the UTM zone 10 projection using the North American Datum of 1983. d_{16}: grain size diameter in millimeters, where 16% of the sample is finer by volume. d_{50}: grain size diameter in millimeters, where 50% of the sample is finer by volume. d_{84}: grain size diameter in millimeters, where 84% of the sample is finer by volume. Location names are informal descriptions of bars based on local landmarks.]

Sample ID	Location	River kilometer	Floodplain kilometer	Easting	Northing	Sample Type	d_{16}	d_{50}	d_{84}
12a	Tidewater Estuary Bar	3.5	2.9	396039	4658364	surface	1.80	17.26	45.00
						subsurface	0.89	7.17	31.29
12b	Tidewater Estuary Bar; mid-bar	3.4	2.9	395999	4658335	surface	3.87	16.18	38.50
12c	Tidewater Estuary Bar; bar toe	3.3	2.8	395903	4658268	surface	3.45	11.91	28.42

   Subsurface samples were collected to assess the difference between the bed surface and subsurface textures (a measure of "armoring") and to support transport calculations with substrate-based bed-material transport equations. Subsurface samples at the bar-apex surface-sample measurement sites were collected from three bars—Fitzhugh Bar (FPkm 15.7), Social Security Bar (FPkm 6.0), and Tidewater Estuary Bar (FPkm 3.0) (table 4). Each subsurface sample was collected by removing the surface layer, consisting approximately of the depth equivalent to the median surface particle diameter, and then collecting 15–20 L from an excavation approximately 40 cm deep and 20 cm in diameter. Subsurface-sample masses ranged from 33 to 39 kg, and are probably not large enough to adequately characterize the distribution of clasts greater than 64 mm (Church and others, 1987; Kondolf and others, 2003). These samples were dried, sieved, and weighed by the USGS sediment laboratory in Vancouver Washington. For each of the subsurface samples, there was one clast in the largest size bin, accounting for 15 percent, 5 percent, and 2 percent of the samples at Fitzhugh Bar, Social Security Bar, and Tidewater Estuary Bar, respectively. For Fitzhugh Bar in particular, this single large 128–256 mm clast forms a relatively large proportion of the total sample, possibly biasing the gradation curve to larger values and resulting in a calculated d_{50} (and other percentile) values larger than would be derived from a larger sample, which would presumably have a relatively smaller volume in the largest size categories.

Assessment of Bed-Material Sizes

   For all the mainstem Chetco River bar-apex surface samples, the median particle diameter (D_{50}) ranges from 57 mm to 17 mm (fig. 22). The three tributary samples were also bracketed by this range. The surface material size distributions show a trend of coarsening between FPkm 14.5 and the confluence of the North Fork Chetco River at FPkm 7.6, followed by fining towards the estuary (FPkm 3). For the three bars with multiple surface samples, median particle size decreases by approximately 30–50 percent along the length of the individual bars (fig. 23). The bar apices appear to also show bimodal size gradations, as the apex sites have similar or greater amounts of fine sediments (less than 10 mm) than the distal bar sites, probably owing to sand and fine gravel deposition on these typically lower elevation sites by waning or later smaller flows after bar mobilization events.

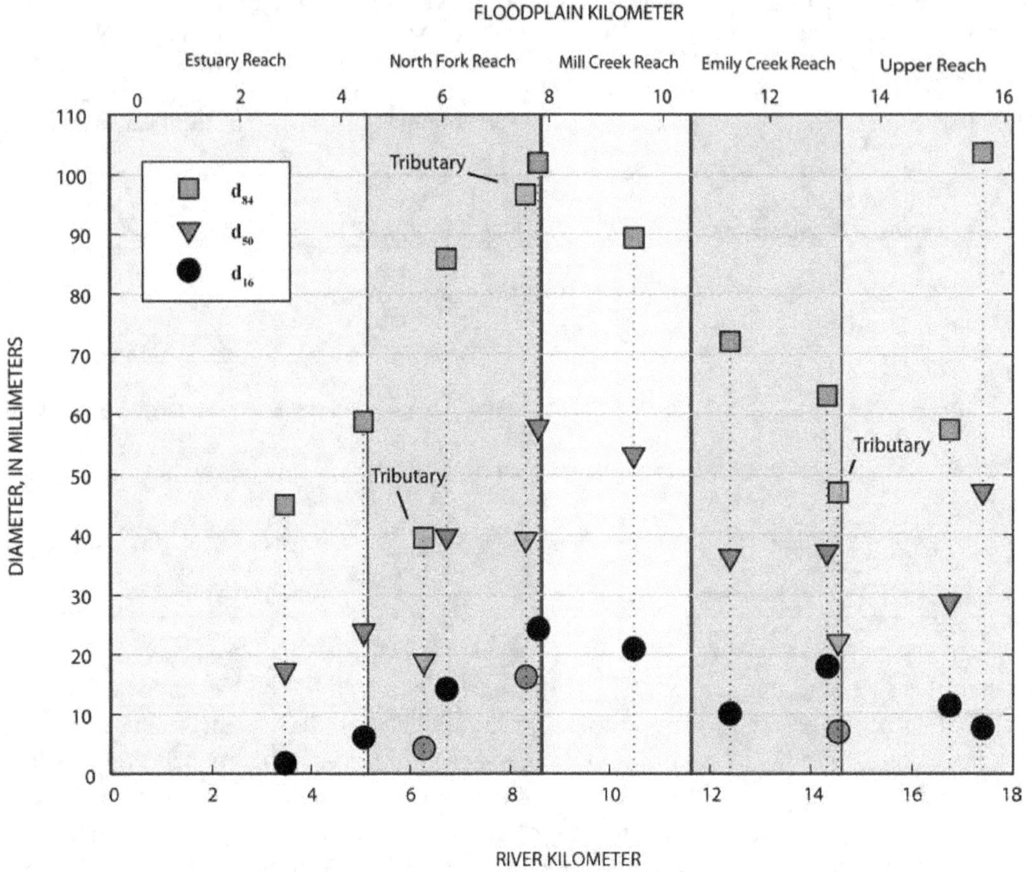

Figure 22. Graph showing longitudinal variation in surface-particle size for bar apices along the Chetco River, Oregon, study area. Surface material was sampled at 12 mainstem Chetco River gravel bars and 3 tributary channels using Wolman (1954) particle count procedure with measurement template.

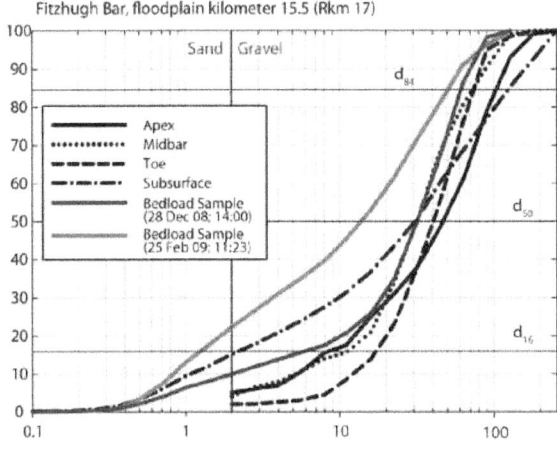

Fitzhugh Bar, floodplain kilometer 15.5 (Rkm 17)

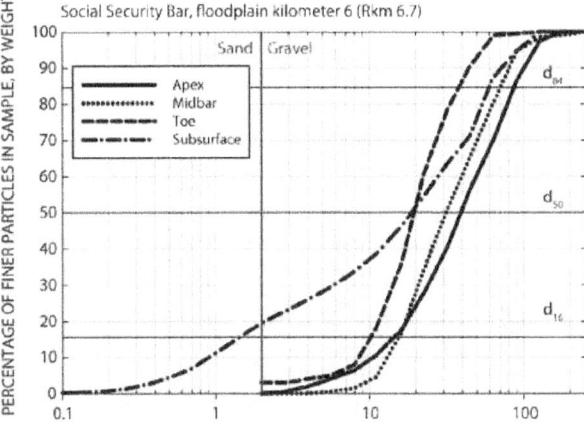

Social Security Bar, floodplain kilometer 6 (Rkm 6.7)

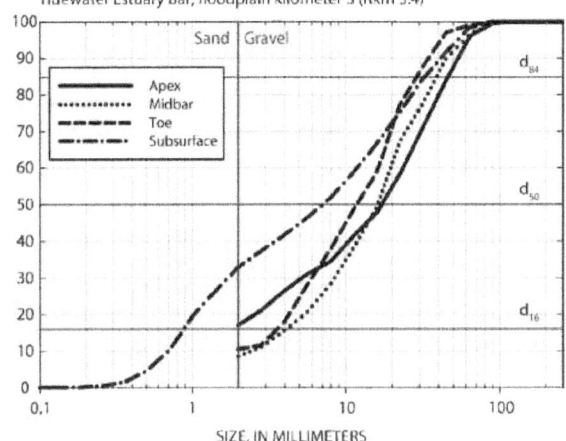

Tidewater Estuary Bar, floodplain kilometer 3 (Rkm 3.4)

Figure 23. Graphs showing particle size distributions for surface and subsurface samples at Fitzhugh Bar, (floodplain kilometer 15.5), Social Security Bar (floodplain kilometer 6.7), and Tidewater Estuary Bar (floodplain kilometer 3), Chetco River, Oregon. At each bar, surface material was sampled at three locations along the bar axis: bar apex, midbar, and toe of bar using Wolman (1954) particle count procedure with

measurement template. Subsurface material sampled volumetrically at bar apex and sieved by USGS sediment laboratory in Vancouver, Washington. Bedload sample size distributions for December 28, 2008, and February 25, 2009, sampling trips shown for comparison with the surface and subsurface samples from the nearby Fitzhugh Bar. Bedload samples analyzed by USGS sediment laboratory in Vancouver.

The three subsurface samples were substantially finer than the surface-material samples measured at the same locations (fig. 23). Previous studies have shown that the relative coarseness of the surface layer increases as a function of the excess transport capacity and that reaches where sediment supply exceeds transport capacity should have little to no armoring, whereas reaches with excess capacity would display increasing levels of armoring (Dietrich and others, 1989; Buffington and Montgomery, 1999). Although the exact relations are uncertain, the degree of armoring (defined as the ratio of d_{50} surface material to d_{50} substrate) can be used as an indication of sediment supply relative to transport capacity (Bunte and Abt, 2001). In general, armoring ratios close to 1 indicate high sediment supply, whereas channels with excess transport capacity typically have armoring ratios greater than 2 (Bunte and Abt, 2001). On the Chetco River, armoring ratios at Fitzhugh Bar, Social Security Bar, and Tidewater Estuary Bar were 1.52, 2.09, and 2.41 respectively, indicating high sediment supply relative to transport conditions at the upstream end of the study reach (although the Fitzhugh Bar armoring ratio may actually be higher if the subsurface sample is biased as described above) but perhaps excess transport capacity relative to sediment supply in the North Fork and Estuary Reaches. The increasing ratio of median surface layer diameter to subsurface median diameter is also counter to typical conditions where armoring ratios decrease with channel slope (Pitlick and others, 2008), a possible indication of downstream changes in sediment supply relative to transport capacity.

Bed Material Lithology and Sources

An important component of the overall sediment budget is the volume of material entering the study reach by tributaries. At the upstream end of the study reach, the contributing drainage area is 702 km^2, 77 percent of the total basin area at the mouth. The largest tributaries are Emily Creek (FPkm 13.2, drainage area 32 km^2), North Fork Chetco River (FPkm 7.6, drainage area 104 km^2), and Jack Creek (FPkm 5.8, drainage area 22 km^2), together accounting for 158 km^2 of the 211 km^2 of drainage area gained by the Chetco River through the study reach. All three of these tributaries have small fans at their junction with the mainstem Chetco River that have episodically grown and eroded, indicating that bed material is entering from these tributary catchments. The simplest approach to estimating the volume of bed material entering by the tributaries is to assume that it is proportional to contributing area. However, this assumption fails to account for possibly different sediment production rates within the drainage basin owing to geology, physiography, and land use (Maguire, 2001). To independently assess the contributions of tributaries, clast lithology at all sites of particle size analysis were evaluated, taking advantage of the distinct geologic terranes contributing sediment to different parts of the drainage basin.

For all bed-material size measurements, we classified clasts greater than 11 mm according to lithology. The lithologic classifications used in this study were not complete identifications traceable to specific geologic units, but simple categories facilitating rapid and consistent hand sample identification. A total of 16 lithologic categories were developed, but 3 of these categories—quartzite (metasandstone), sandstone, and basalt—dominated the total assemblage of particles sampled. Surface material was classified in the field during the particle size counts, and lithologies of subsurface material were determined on the sieved samples after size analysis by the USGS sediment laboratory.

The dominant clast type for all mainstem sampling sites was a dark grey and very hard metasedimentary rock designated as "quartzite," composing 50–80 percent of most mainstem samples (fig. 24), followed by fine- to coarse-grained lithic sandstones typically composing 20–40 percent of the sampled clasts. Both of these clast types are likely derived mainly from the Dothan Formation, which underlies the western half of the drainage basin, and enter the study reach from upstream as well as from tributaries. Several clast types are unique to the upper drainage basin and the mainstem Chetco River at the upper end of the study reach, including coarse-grained igneous and metamorphic rock, and ultramafic rocks, but they typically compose less than 10 percent of the sampled rock types. We sampled bed material at the three major tributaries, Emily Creek, North Fork Chetco River, and Jack Creek, for which the percentage of sandstone was greater than for most of the mainstem sample sites.

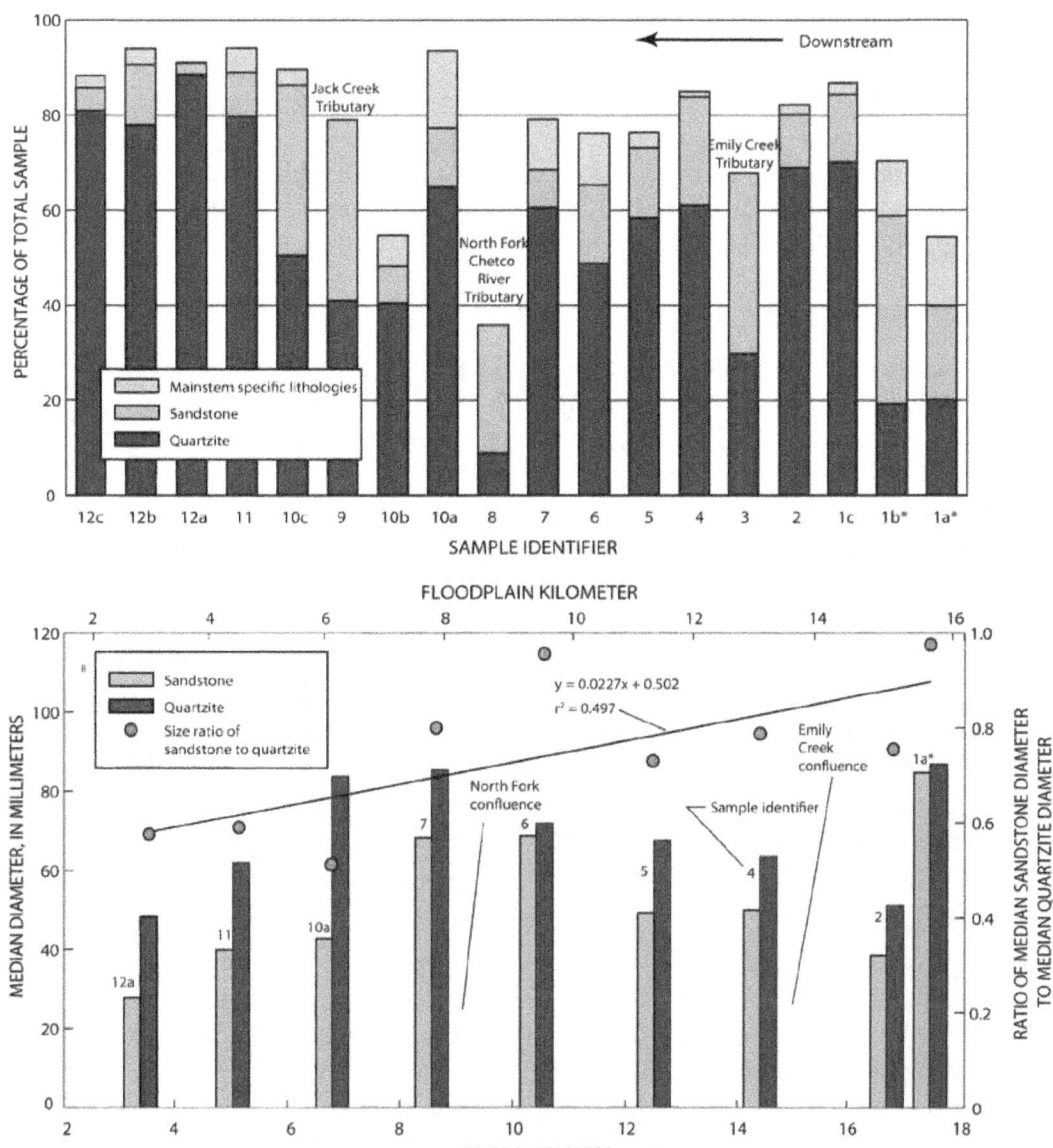

Figure 24. Graphs showing variation in clast lithology and size ratio of sandstone and quartzite clasts for sites along the Chetco River, Oregon, study area. A. Variation in clast lithology for each of the 18 surface-material samples taken from 12 bars along the mainstem Chetco River and 3 tributary bars. Sample locations reported in table 4, but locations proceed downstream in order of sample identifier. Samples 1b and 1a done with slightly different protocol, so results not directly comparable. Totals do not sum to 100 percent because unidentified and minor local clast types are not included. B. Median diameter (d_{50}) of sandstone and quartzite particles at each of the mainstem Chetco sites where surface material was sampled, and downstream trend in the ratios of median diameters. The ratios of sandstone to quartzite d_{50} at each site indicate a general downstream trend of decreasing sandstone size relative to quartzite size.

The small number of distinctly upper-basin classes and their variation among samples precludes strong inferences regarding the contribution of bed material by the tributaries except that the presence of these clast types in relatively similar percentages all the way to the estuary indicates that the bed material brought in by tributaries is not a substantial percentage of the sampled distributions. A mixing model analysis of the ratio of sandstones to quartzites applied to samples from Emily Creek and North

Fork Chetco River with adjacent mainstem samples indicates that the North Fork contributes up to 7 percent of the total bed-material volume at its confluence (compared to the 12 percent of the total basin area at the confluence), and that Emily Creek contributes 7–31 percent at its confluence (compared to the 4.4 percent of the total basin area at the confluence), although these values are highly sensitive to the choice of local mainstem distributions. Given the ranges permitted by this analysis, it is assumed that bed material sediment influx from tributaries is related to drainage area, indicating that about 25 percent of the bed material in the study reach is contributed by local tributaries.

Bed-material Particle Attrition

In opposition to the bed material introduced by tributaries is the wearing down of bed material by fracture, abrasion, dissolution, and weathering as it moves downstream. Particle attrition reduces bed material sediment volumes because some of the finer particles created by mechanical breakage will become part of the suspended load that leaves the active channel environment for either overbank floodplain deposition or the Pacific Ocean. Primary evidence for such attrition is the downstream fining of bed material typically seen in gravel-bed rivers (Mackin, 1948; Schumm and Stevens, 1973), made stronger by instances of differential fining of distinct clast lithologies (Plumley, 1948; Shaw and Kellerhals, 1982; Kodama, 1994). Many studies, however, have shown that such fining results chiefly from sorting by selective deposition (Paola and others, 1992; Hoey and Ferguson, 1994; Rice 1999). For the Chetco River, a decreasing trend in the size of sandstone clasts relative to quartzite clasts in the downstream direction indicates some particle breakdown (fig. 24). Although complicated by many factors such as the introduction of tributary sandstone clasts, the approximately 40 percent reduction in particle diameter for the sandstone clasts relative to quartz would indicate nearly an 80 percent volume reduction of sandstone. If the sandstone clasts were the only clast type with significant attrition, the volume reduction of the gravel would be less than 10–20 percent given the small percentage of sandstone composing the greater than 11mm sediment.

We also assess downstream volume loss by applying the attrition coefficients provided by (1) Shaw and Kellerhals (1982) for the fractional diameter reduction of quartzites in natural rivers of 0.0017/km, giving an volume reduction of 5.5 percent for length of channel between FPkm 15 and 5; and (2) the experimental tumbler results by Collins and Dunne (1989) for Olympic Peninsula rocks that indicate fractional diameter reduction rates equating to a 10–30 percent volumetric reduction by abrasion between FPkm 15 and 5. We judge the Collins and Dunne (1989) attrition rates to be the maximum plausible volumetric reduction because of the likely greater hardness of the Chetco River bed materials. Taken together, we judge the volumetric bed-material attrition rate along the length of the Chetco River study reach to be between 5 and 30 percent.

Flow Modeling

The driver of bed-material transport is streamflow, including the temporal sequence of high flows over the years and the spatial distribution of hydraulic conditions along the channel. The sequence of past flows for the Chetco River comes from records of the USGS streamflow measurement station at FPkm 15.2 (fig. 2). To determine the spatial distribution of hydraulic conditions produced by this range of flows on the Chetco River, we constructed a one-dimensional hydraulic model of the study reach. The results from this model support the equation-based predictions of bed-material transport described subsequently.

For the Chetco River study area, we applied the Hydrologic Engineering Center's River Analysis System (HEC-RAS) Version 4.0 model (U.S. Army Corps of Engineers, 2006). The HEC-RAS model calculates one-dimensional (cross section averaged) energy-balanced water surface profiles for a series of cross sections and specified discharges and energy loss coefficients. Calculated values include cross-section-average water-surface elevations and energy slopes (S_f) for each cross section. For applications in subcritical flow regimes, calculations proceed upstream.

For this analysis, valley-bottom geometry was defined using 68 cross sections between FPkm 0.5 and FPkm 15.5. Cross sections spanned the entire valley bottom and were spaced at intervals approximately equal to the active channel width (typically about 300 m), but with a maximum spacing of 900 m. The cross sections were developed from the LIDAR merged with bathymetric surveys, both from 2008, and from streamflow measurement surveys at the USGS streamflow measurement station. The upstream-stepping flow computations for each simulated discharge were started at normal depth at the downstream cross section at FPkm 0.5. Discharge was assumed to increase by 14 percent at the North Fork Chetco River confluence at FPkm 7.6, consistent with incremental area contributed by this basin relative to the drainage area at the upstream end of the reach. Flow from other tributaries entering the Chetco River within the study area was not considered because the North Fork Chetco River is the only tributary basin with large enough area likely to contribute significant discharge at, or near, the same time that discharge in the mainstem Chetco River is peaking.

The HEC-RAS model was calibrated by comparing the calculated water-surface elevations to the rating curve in use during the summer of 2008 at the USGS Chetco River streamflow measurement station at FPkm 15.2 near the upstream end of the modeled reach. A suitable fit resulted from applying Mannings n values of 0.04 to the channel bed and banks for the entire study reach. The calculated profiles from this model closely match the water-surface profile determined from the LIDAR survey of 2008, when flow was approximately 7.8 m^3/s according to the stage-discharge relation at the USGS gage, as well as water-surface elevations during the December 29, 2008, flow of 1,440 m^3/s. From this calibrated model, water-surface elevation and S_f were calculated for each of the 68 cross sections and for 20 discharges ranging between 5.5 and 2,270 m^3/s, encompassing the range of flows likely to transport bed material as well as all recorded flood peaks since 1970 (fig. 25).

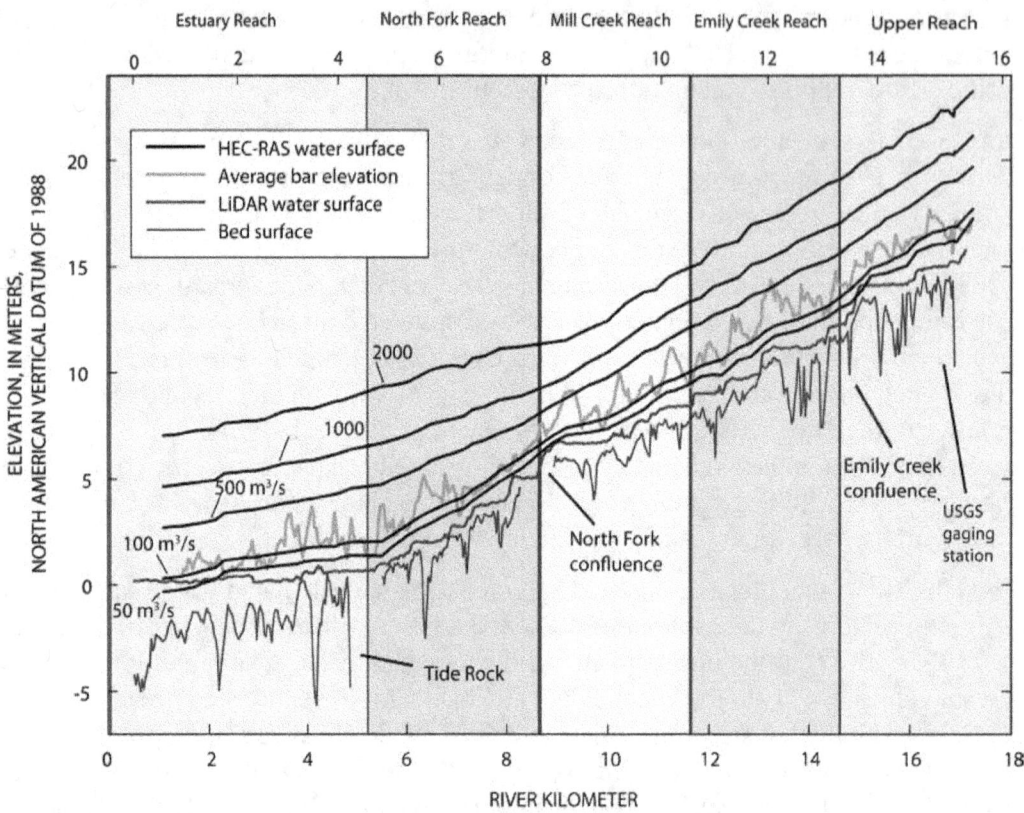

Figure 25. Graph showing surveyed channel thalweg in 2008 (USGS survey), water-surface (from LIDAR, discharge approximately 7.8 cubic meters per second), bar surfaces (from LIDAR), and calculated water-surface profiles for flows between 50 and 2,000 cubic meters per second for the lower Chetco River, Oregon.

The calculated water-surface and energy profiles generally match the thalweg and low-flow water-surface profiles, but become more regular with increasing discharge (fig. 25). This transformation owes to the decreasing influence of channel morphology, such as pool-and-riffle geometry, and increasing influence of overall valley geometry on flow hydraulics as discharge increases. Because of the specified downstream boundary condition of normal depth, the modeling results do not account for the approximately 2 m tidal range affecting the Estuary Reach, which has a significant effect on low flows but is unlikely to affect mean sediment transport conditions during high flows. All profiles show a gradient inflection: For low flows, this corresponds to the upstream limit of tidal influence and a slight change in thalweg slope near FPkm 5; for higher flows, this inflection moves upstream into the Mill Creek Reach, approaching FPkm 10 for flows of 2,000 m³/s, corresponding to the significant increase in valley-bottom width near the North Fork confluence. This change in slope has important implications for reach-scale bed-material transport. The flow modeling also shows that most bars are inundated by flows of 250–500 m³/s.

Direct Measurement of Bedload Transport

Although challenging and subject to many uncertainties, direct measurement of bedload transport can substantially aid estimates of annual fluxes of bed material (Hicks and Gomez, 2003). An ideal situation is to make numerous bedload transport measurements over a range of flows so as to produce a bedload rating curve relating bedload transport rates to river flow (for example, Emmett, 1980; Wilcock and others, 1996; Pitlick and others, 2008). This process requires multiple measurements, possibly over several years to encompass the necessary range of flows, and is especially difficult for rivers such as the Chetco River in which sediment transporting flows are in response to short duration rainfall events. As a consequence, the purpose of making bedload measurements on the Chetco River was not to develop a bedload transport rating curve but solely to aid in selection of bedload transport equations as described in the following sections. The measurements reported here, however, could be incorporated into a bedload rating curve as part of a sustained measurement program.

Sampling

Two measurement trips were completed during winter 2008–09. The measurements were made from the bridge crossing the river at the USGS streamflow measurement site at FPkm 15.2, near the upstream boundary of the study reach. The channel here makes a sweeping left bend, with the low flow channel abutting steep bedrock of the valley wall, and the left side formed by an active gravel bar inset against vegetated floodplain. For sampling, we used an 80 kg TR-2 bedload sampler with a 30-cm-wide by 15-cm-tall opening with a 0.5 mm mesh collection bag (fig. 26). The TR-2 sampler was designed by the USGS in 1986 to sample coarse sand and gravel in the vicinity of Mount St. Helens after the 1980 eruption (Childers, 1992), and has size and weight characteristics appropriate for the high flows and coarse sediment loads typical of the Chetco River. The sampler was suspended from the bridge with a truck-mounted hydraulic winch. The nose of the sampler was stabilized by a line running through a wheeled pulley riding a stay line crossing the river approximately 30 m upstream, with the free end controlled by personnel on the bridge deck.

Figure 26. Photographs showing bedload sampling at USGS streamflow gaging station Chetco River near Brookings, Oregon (14400000), Chetco River, Oregon, December 28, 2008. Streamflow was 1,170 cubic meters per second. (Photographs by Jim O'Connor, U.S. Geological Survey, December 28, 2008.) A. View of sampling equipment, including truck and sampler, during deployment; cable in view is for discharge measurements and was not used for bedload sampling. B. TR-2 sampler after sample collection.

Sampling protocols were modified from the single-equal-width-method prescribed by Edwards and Glysson (1999) to account for time limitations. For each sampling transect, the cross section was sampled by 8–10 verticals [in contrast to the 20–40 verticals recommended by Edwards and Glysson (1999)] spaced at 4.6–6.1 m apart. The sampler was placed on the bed for 30 seconds for each sample. The intent was to make multiple transects for each measurement, but time and equipment limitations allowed only one complete (or nearly complete) transect for each measurement. The sampler was emptied after most individual vertical measurements, except for near the flow edges where there was little material collected. Samples were dried, weighed and sieved by the U.S. Geological Survey Sediment Laboratory in Vancouver, Washington (table 5). Transport rates were calculated by

$$Q_b = M \times \frac{\left[\frac{W}{(n \times w)}\right]}{T},$$

(1)

where Q_b is the bedload transport in kilograms per second, M is the sample mass in kilograms, T is the sample time (for each vertical) in seconds, W is the wetted width in meters, n is the number of verticals, and w is the width of the sampler in meters.

Table 5. Summary of bedload measurements for winter 2008–09, Chetco River, Oregon

[Measurements at U.S. Geological Survey streamflow measurement station 14400000 with TR-2 sampler; using modified version of single equal-width-increment method of Edwards and Glysson (1999). Abbreviations: kg, kilograms; mm, millimeters; m^3/s, cubic meters per second, m, meters; kg/s, kilograms per second; --, no data]

Sample transect (date and start time)	Number of verticals	Sample mass (kg)	Median particle size (mm)	Water discharge (m^3/s)	Channel width (m)	Bedload discharge (kg/s)	Comments
12/28/2008 at 11:00	10	102.4	31	1,190	70	78.4	Poor sampler contact with channel bed for some verticals
12/28/2008 at 14:00	10	193.9	13	1,120	70	148.4	Good sampler contact with channel bed for most verticals
2/24/2009 at 11:23	9	21.6	0.8	290	60	15.7	Sampler support cable failed at vertical 8; calculation assumes no material for verticals 8 and 9, so this should be considered a minimum value

The first measurement trip was December 28–29, 2008, during a wet storm producing high flows along the southern Oregon coast. Flow on the Chetco River rose from about 105 m^3/s early on December 27 to a peak of 1,200 m^3/s at 12:15 on December 28, before decreasing to about 880 m^3/s by midnight of December 28. Flow then rose again, peaking even higher at 12:15 on December 29 with a discharge of 1,450 m^3/s. For comparison, the 2-year and 5-year recurrence-interval flows on the Chetco River are 1,060 and 1,425 m^3/s respectively (fig. 27). During these flows, depths exceeded 12 m and surface velocities were greater than 3 m/s. Two measurement transects were completed on December

28. The first, between 11:00 and 13:10, spanned the peak flow for the day. Because it was difficult to maintain the stability of the sampler in the water and to be certain that it was securely on the channel bed (severe drag on the supporting cable and stay-line prevented detectable slackening of the support cable when the sampler grounded), this measurement is considered inferior to the second measurement of the day, between 14:00 and 16:06, in which the sampler maintained better position and contact with the bed. An attempted measurement during the higher flow of December 29 was unsuccessful because the velocities and flow depths prohibited the sampler from reaching the channel bottom in a controlled manner.

The second measurement trip was on February 24, 2009, in the midst of several days of elevated flow following a late winter frontal system that crossed the Chetco River drainage basin. Flow rose from less than 30 m^3/s early on February 21 to a peak of 450 m^3/s at 18:00 on February 23 before dropping overnight. During the February 24 sampling between 11:23 and 12:17, flow was steady at 290 m^3/s for the entire measurement period (fig. 27). This flow has been exceeded on a mean daily basis for 4.4 percent of the period October 1, 1969–March 5, 2009. For this bedload measurement, with much less intense flow than the December 28–29 event, sampling proceeded well, with solid contact with the bed, until the 8th (and penultimate) vertical near the right bank, when the sampler support cable failed, halting completion of the transect. The partial results are reported in table 5 and the calculated transport rate should be considered a minimum value, although the two missing verticals would add negligibly to the total judging from (1) the relative contribution of load from that part of the cross section during the December 28 measurements, (2) the trend of sample masses from this transect, and (3) acoustic Doppler "moving bed" measurements made later in the day (fig. 28).

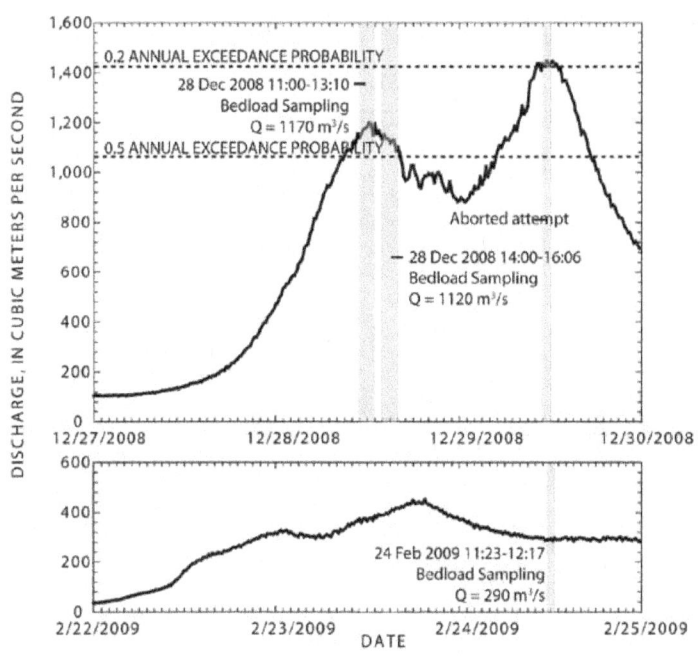

Figure 27. Graphs showing flow and sampling periods for bedload measurements on the Chetco River, Oregon. A. December 29–30, 2008, sampling periods, also showing flow exceedance probabilities as calculated following Bulletin 17 guidelines from annual peak flows for the period 1970–2007. B. February 24–25, 2009, sampling period.

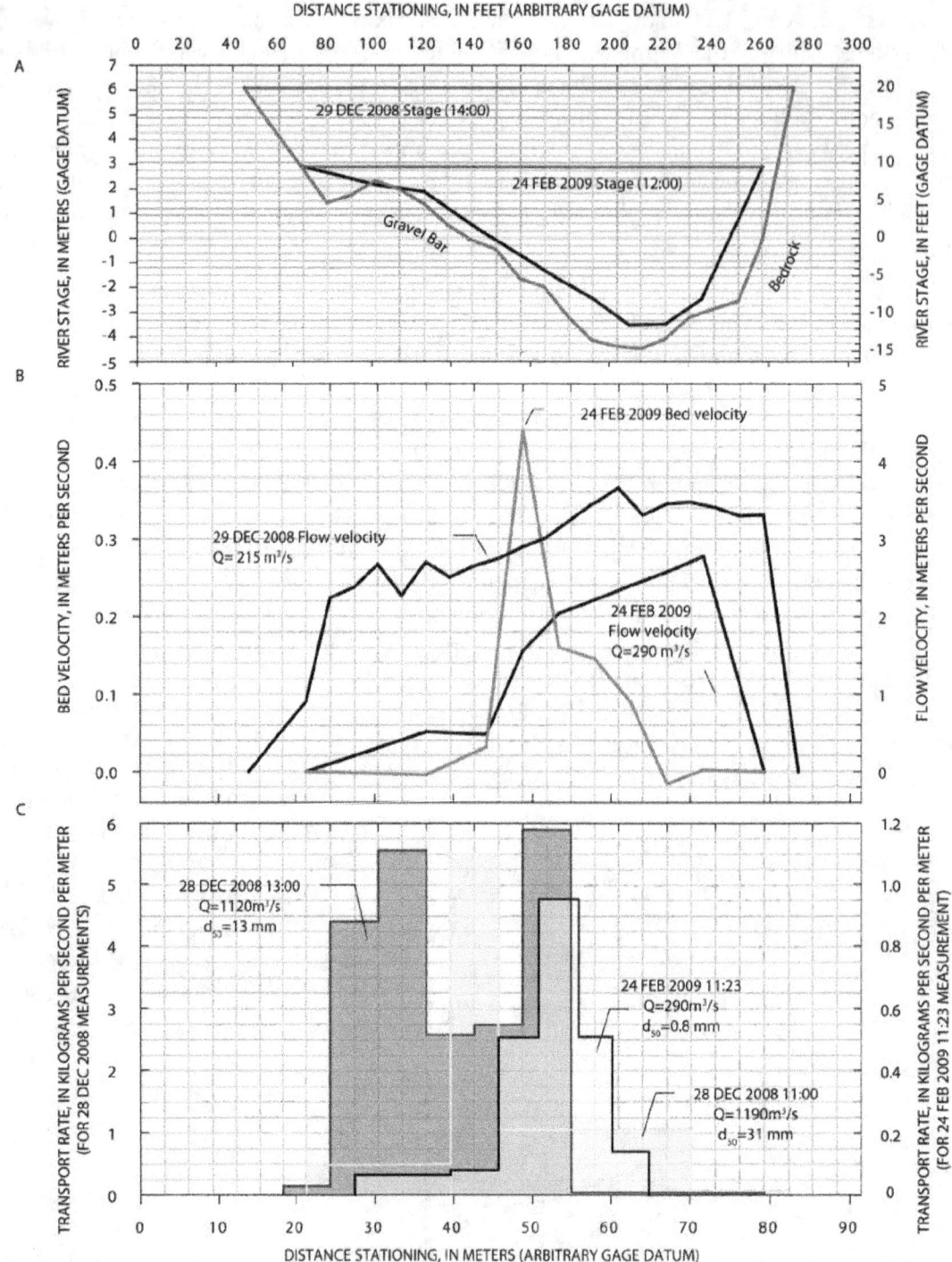

Figure 28. Graphs showing summary flow and bedload transport data for December 28–30, 2008, and February 24–25, 2009, measurements, Chetco River, Oregon. A. Channel cross-sections, from December 29–30, 2008, and February 24–25. 2009, soundings, with measured water surface elevations. B. Depth-averaged mean velocity from 29 December 29, 2008, and February 24, 2009, measurements, and February 24 moving-bed velocity, as measured by acoustic Doppler current profiler. C. Measured unit bedload transport rates by sampling vertical; several verticals were composited for the December 28, 2008, 11:00 measurement, reducing spatial resolution. Bulk of transport for this measurement was between stations 40 and 55.

Results and Discussion of Bedload Sampling

Despite the sampling difficulties and incomplete results, the measurements show high rates of coarse bedload transport at high flows (fig. 28, table 5). The transport rate for the December 28 14:00 measurement, corresponding to a flow slightly exceeding the 2-year recurrence-interval discharge, was nearly 150 kg/s, with an average unit transport rate of 2.1 kg/m/s. As expected, the transport rate of the lower flow of February 24, 2009, was much lower—only 15.7 kg/s and a unit transport rate of 0.26 kg/m/s. The transport rate calculated from the December 28 14:00 measurement is higher than nearly all reported examples of high bed load transport rates on western U.S. gravel-bed stream and rivers—which typically range up to about 0.4 kg/m/s—but is less than the 3.9 kg/m/s measured for the North Fork Toutle River in a drainage basin tremendously disturbed by the 1980 Mount St. Helens eruption (Pitlick, 1992; Pitlick and others, 2009). The measured transport rate at the highest flow, 1,190 m³/s, was substantially lower than the one later in the day at a slightly lower flow, but this owes to poor sampler contact with the bed for several of the measurement verticals. Evident from all measurements, including the "moving bed" Doppler measurement also made on February 24, 2009, is that most bed-load transport was over the gravel bar forming the left bank, despite higher velocities in the channel thalweg (fig. 28).

The median particle size of the bedload scaled with water discharge, with the median particle size for the December 28, 2008, measurements ranging from 13 to 31 mm, whereas sediment collected during the February 24, 2009, high flow was chiefly sand with a median diameter of 0.9 mm. The D_{84} for the December 28, 2008, 11:00 and 14:00 measurements were 50 and 60 mm respectively, slightly finer than the 70- to 110-mm D_{84} values for surface and subsurface bed-material samples collected from Fitzhugh bar, 0.5 to 1 km upstream (fig. 29). Although bedload is typically finer than the surface material and is closer in size to subsurface material (Lisle, 1995), it is possible that the TR-2 sampler, with its 152- by 305-mm opening, was undersampling the largest clasts. Alternatively, still higher flows may be required to transport the coarsest particles in this reach.

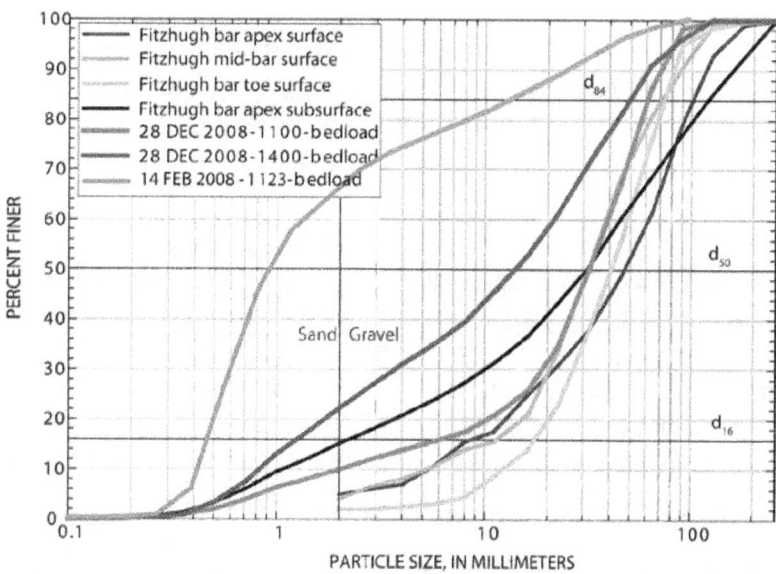

Figure 29. Graph showing particle size distributions for sampled bedload and Fitzhugh Bar (floodplain kilometer 15.5) surface and subsurface measurement, Chetco River, Oregon. Bedload and Fitzhugh Bar subsurface gradations from sieve analysis by USGS sediment laboratory in Vancouver, Washington; surface gradations from Wolman (1954) particle count with measurement template.

Estimation of Bed-Material Transport Rates Using Established Transport Equations

Application of bed-material transport formulas are a common means of estimating sediment fluxes in streams (Collins and Dunne, 1989; Gomez, 1991; Hicks and Gomez, 2003). A primary advantage of using bedload transport equations is that the approach can be applied on any stream for which information on flow, channel geometry and bed-sediment characteristics is available. Moreover, the application of these formulas is typically straightforward and can provide a relatively rapid means of estimating sediment flux across a range of flow scenarios, from individual storm events to decades. For the Chetco River, we apply multiple transport relations for seven locations between FPkm 15.3 and 2.6 for the nearly 40 years of available flow data, enabling assessment of spatial and temporal trends in bed-material transport.

Although there are several empirical and semiempirical transport equations for bedload transport (Gomez and Church, 1989), all actually predict only the transport capacity, defined as the "maximum load a river can carry" (Gilbert and Murphy, 1914, p. 35). For conditions of unlimited bed material available from the bed and banks, a correct relation for transport capacity coupled with accurate descriptions of flow and bed material should result in accurate estimates of bed-material flux. For the Chetco River, the assumption of unlimited supply is probably approximately valid because of the voluminous gravel accumulations flanking and underlying the valley bottom within the study area and in the 12 km upstream of the study area.

Nonetheless, even if river conditions meet this requirement that bed-material transport is a function of flow, channel, and bed texture rather than sediment availability, large uncertainties still arise because bed-material transport is highly variable in time and governed by highly nonlinear relations between local flow and bed material tranport—both of which are difficult to characterize at high resolution (Gomez, 1991; Wilcock and others, 2009). These challenges, in conjunction with the wide variety of field situations and few measurements, in part explain the large number of transport equations available and the variation in their forms and data requirements (Hicks and Gomez, 2003). For this study, we assess and possibly mitigate for these factors by (1) evaluating multiple transport relations for multiple cross sections, (2) check transport equations against the direct bedload measurements, (3) characterize flow at individual cross sections using the results from a calibrated one-dimensional flow model, and (4) evaluate the results in the context of other information on sediment flux rates.

Equation Selection and Analysis

The bedload transport calculations for the Chetco River were implemented by the software package Bedload Assessment in Gravel-bedded Streams (BAGS), a program operating within a Microsoft Excel workbook (Pitlick and others, 2009). BAGS enables users to select from six semiempirical transport formulas, all of which were developed and tested using data from gravel or sandy-gravel streams (Wilcock and others, 2009). Users specify an equation and geometry, flow, and sediment parameters. With this information, bed-material transport rates are calculated for a specific flow and cross section geometry.

The bedload transport formulas implemented in BAGS are:

- Parker–Klingeman–McLean, a substrate-based equation (Parker and others, 1982)

- Parker–Klingeman, a substrate-based equation (Parker and Klingeman, 1982)

- Bakke and others, a calibrated equation version of the Parker–Klingeman formula (Bakke and others, 1999)

- Parker, a surface-based equation (Parker, 1990 a,b)

- Wilcock, a two-fraction calibrated model for sand and gravel, (Wilcock, 2001)

- Wilcock and Crowe, a surface based equation (Wilcock and Crowe, 2003)

Although all six formulas are substantively similar and have been successfully applied to gravel-bed rivers, key attributes differentiate the equations, elaborated in Wilcock and others (2009). The substrate-based methods (Parker-Klingeman-McLean and Parker-Klingeman) rely upon grain size data from the bed subsurface, and were developed using data collected by Milhous (1973) at Oak Creek, a small gravel-bed stream in the Oregon Coast Range. There are two surface-based methods; the Parker (1990 a, b) equation was developed from grain-size distributions and transport rates at Oak Creek, whereas the Wilcock and Crowe (2003) equation was developed from flume experiments using varying amounts of sand. The two calibrated equations of Bakke and others (1999) and Wilcock (2001) require measurements of bedload transport in order to calibrate reference shear stress, and thus improve the overall transport estimates. In this study, four of the six bedload equations in BAGS were applied to the Chetco River; the two calibrated models of Bakke and others (1999) and Wilcock (2001) equation were not used because of too few direct bedload measurements for reliable calibration.

For the Chetco River, we first applied the four equations not requiring calibration to a cross section adjacent to the bedload measurement site to enable comparison with the direct bedload measurements collected during winter 2008–09 (fig. 30). Underlying the resulting calculations are the surface and subsurface bed-material size distributions measured near the cross section, channel cross sections from the HEC–RAS model, a range of modeled streamflows and their associated model-calculated energy-slope (S_f) values. Although all four equations overpredict the measured transport value for the higher quality December 28, 2008, 14:00 measurement at a streamflow of 1,120 m^3/s by a factor of 1.7 to 3.8, the Parker (1990a, b) and Wilcock and Crowe (2003) surface-bed-composition equations performed better in closely predicting the transport rate measured for the 290 m^3/s streamflow of February 24, 2009 (fig. 28).

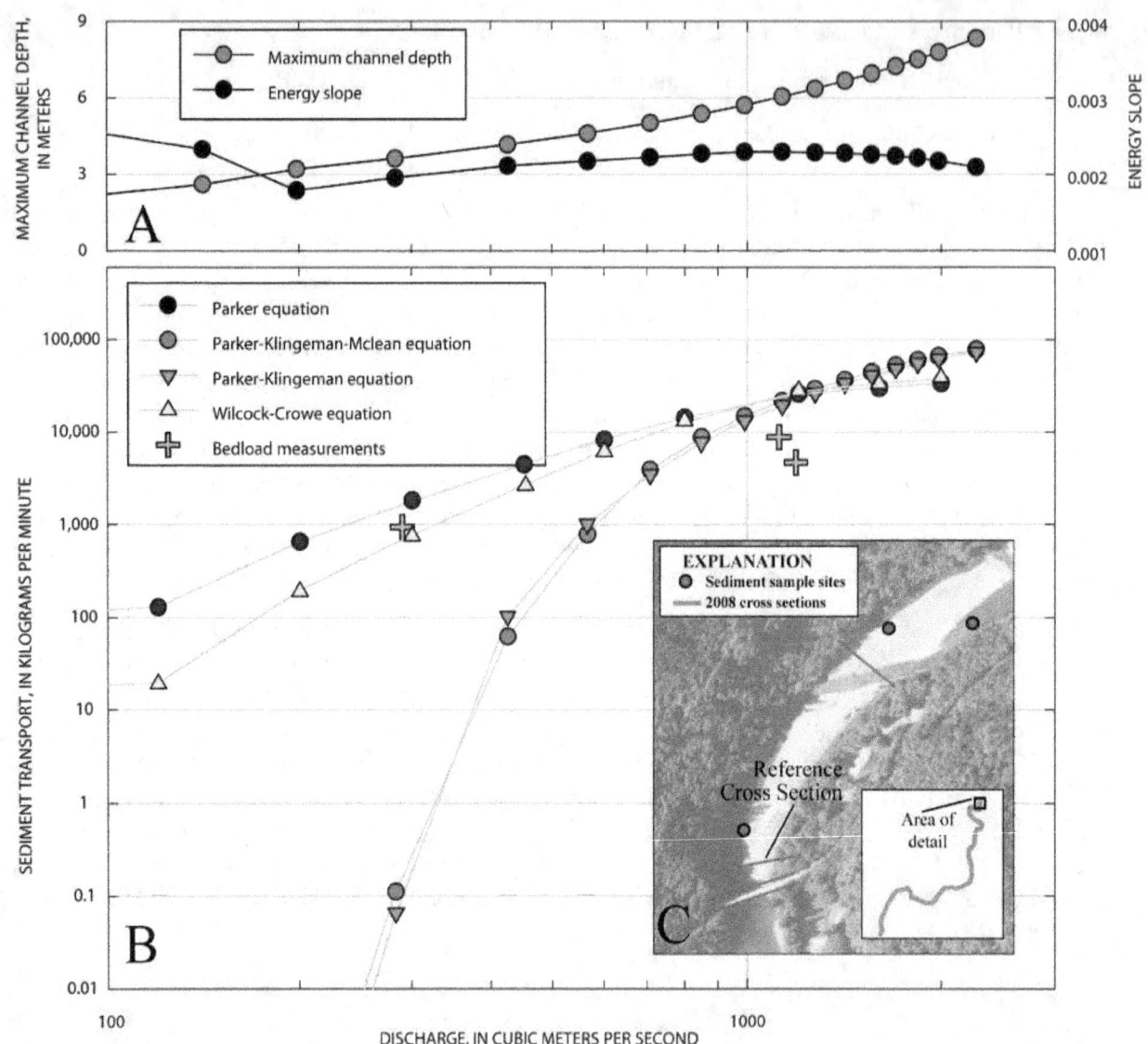

Figure 30. Graphs and map showing streamflow hydraulics, predicted and measured bed-material transport, and location map for vicinity of measurement site near river kilometer 15.3 or the Chetco River, Oregon. A. Modeled flow depth and energy slope for reference cross section at floodplain kilometer 15.3. B. Predicted bed-material transport rates at reference cross section at floodplain kilometer 15.3 for four bed-material transport equations described in text. Also shown are measured bedload transport rates for three measurements made from bridge at floodplain kilometer 15.24. C. Location of streamflow-model cross sections, bed-material transport calculations (reference cross section), the bridge from which the bedload measurements were made (which is also the location of the USGS streamflow gaging station), and location of sediment samples from which grain-size measurements were averaged for calculating bedload transport rates.

The subsequent analysis was carried forward using only the Parker (1990a, b) and Wilcock and Crowe (2003) bed-material transport relations, which have a similar theoretical framework. The major distinction between the two approaches is in determination of the reference Shields shear stress (τ_{rsg}^*); in the Parker (1990a, b) equation, τ_{rsg}^* is assumed to be a constant value of 0.0386, but in the Wilcock and Crowe (2003) equation, τ_{rsg}^* varies with the sand content of the surface bed material.

For each of 7 cross sections between FPkm 2.6 and FPkm 15.3, we calculated transport rates for 12 discharges ranging between 15 and 2,000 m^3/s, using the model-calculated S_f values and nearby measurements of bar-surface particle size (fig. 30, tables 4 and 6). Discharges were increased by 14 percent at the North Fork confluence to account for tributary inflow. The results for each discharge produced a relation between discharge (Q) and bed-material transport rate (Qs), which were fitted by curves to produce a sediment-discharge rating curve. Although many sediment rating curves are fit by power functions (Hicks and Gomez, 2003; Wilcock and others, 2009), this form did not fully characterize the calculated Chetco River bed-material transport rates. As a consequence, we developed continuous ratings by fitting piecewise polynomial functions to the results for each cross section.

In part, the poor fit of power functions resulted from using the energy slope (S_f) instead of a reach-averaged channel slope. The energy slopes calculated by the step-backwater modeling varied substantially with discharge at nearly all cross sections (fig. 30A), reflecting the transition from channel control on slope (mostly owing to the pool and riffle structure of the low flow channel) to broader valley-bottom controls at higher discharges. Consequently, the transport rating curves were highly variable, especially at low discharges, but approached more typical power functions at higher discharges as S_f approached reach-scale valley slopes (for example fig. 30B).

Partly as a consequence of the nonsystematic variation of S_f with discharge, high transport rates were calculated for some cross sections at very low discharge (commonly where cross sections were located at riffles). In these cases, we assumed no transport at these low discharges. The cutoff discharge ranged from 50 to 230 m^3/s for all but one of the cross sections—flows typically confined to the low flow channel or barely covering low channel-flanking bars and unlikely to transport substantial bed material (fig. 25; Mueller and others, 2005). For the cross section located at FPkm 9.4, no transport was assumed for flows less than 425–450 m^3/s, depending on the transport relation. Very low transport rates calculated for this cross section were likely the result of relatively coarse bed material at the closest sample location, coupled with low calculated energy gradients (table 6).

The resulting Q–Q$_s$ relations served as a basis for calculating annual sediment transport fluxes and their spatial and temporal variation. Annual transport volumes were calculated for each cross section by applying the October 1, 1969–September 30, 2008, discharge record from the USGS streamflow measurement station at FPkm 15.3. Typically, this is done with the mean daily values (for example, Collins and Dunne, 1989) but because of the combination of the highly nonlinear transport rates and the rapid flow changes on the Chetco River during transport events, annual bed-material transport volumes determined from mean daily values are likely to underestimate true values. In consideration of this, we based annual bed-material transport volumes on the higher resolution unit discharge values. For the Chetco River, unit flow values have been recorded at 15-minute intervals since 2006 and at 30-minute intervals prior, but are only electronically archived for the post-1988 period.

Table 6. Summary of calculated transport rates for the Chetco River, Oregon

[Abbreviations: d16, 16th percentile; d50, 50th percentile; d84, 84th percentile; mm, millimeter; kg/s, kilograms per second; Rkm, river kilometer; FPkm, floodplain kilometer; m3/s, cubic meters per second]

Cross Section Location (Rkm)	(FPkm)	d16 (mm)	d50 (mm)	d84 (mm)	%<2m m (%)	Distance to surface sample site (m)	Equation	Low-flow cutoff (m3/s)	Energy slope (50 m3/s)	Transport rate, kg/s	Energy slope (100 m3/s)	Transport rate, kg/s	Energy slope (500 m3/s)	Transport rate, kg/s	Energy slope (1000 m3/s)	Transport rate, kg/s	Energy slope (2000 m3/s)	Transport rate, kg/s	Mean annual transport, 1970–2008 (m3/yr)
16.9	15.3	12.76	38.64	82.80	3.7	250	Parker	150	0.333%	0.246	0.245%	0.293	0.214%	60	0.229%	305	0.217%	568	51,100
							Wilcock-Crowe	50		1.414		1.883		89		306		509	73,900
16.5	14.9	11.86	28.87	57.42	0.0	250	Parker	100	0.035%	0.000	0.060%	1.364	0.180%	98	0.180%	270	0.170%	793	103,200
							Wilcock-Crowe	100		0.000		0.660		47		113		324	54,300
14.6	13.3	18.64	37.15	63.07	1.0	270	Parker	100	0.119%	0.001	0.161%	10.436	0.211%	38	0.183%	167	0.161%	600	79,100
							Wilcock-Crowe	100		0.009		5.630		21		84		278	43,600
12.6	11.5	11.00	36.33	72.13	3.5	180	Parker	230	0.053%	0.000	0.066%	0.000	0.179%	118	0.243%	485	0.248%	789	83,000
							Wilcock-Crowe	170		0.000		0.053		136		444		663	91,100
9.4	8.5	21.78	53.26	89.40	1.0	850	Parker	450	0.036%	0.000	0.059%	0.000	0.143%	4	0.171%	30	0.119%	3	5,700
							Wilcock-Crowe	425		0.000		0.000		4		23		5	4,100
6.0	5.3	10.40	19.75	37.96	3.0	20	Parker	110	0.152%	0.004	0.155%	0.116	0.086%	10	0.083%	78	0.084%	326	9,600
							Wilcock-Crowe	110		0.108		0.673		11		56		189	10,100
3.1	2.6	2.50	11.93	30.10	12.0	240	Parker	230	0.027%	0.000	0.040%	0.000	0.049%	2	0.051%	38	0.063%	310	3,900
							Wilcock-Crowe	100		0.101		0.548		16		99		402	15,100

For the 1988 through 2008 water years, we calculated transport rates for each cross section using the 15-min and 30-min unit flow data, summing total transport for each day. To extend the record back through water year 1970 and to fill more recent periods when unit flow data was not available (unit flow data are not available for all of 1993 and parts of several other years), we developed relations for each cross section between daily transport volumes calculated from the unit flow measurements and mean daily flow for all days of predicted transport. These regressions, which had regression correlation coefficients ranging from 0.968 to 0.998, were applied to all days so to permit calculations for the entire October 1, 1969–September 30, 2008, record.

Results and Discussion of Bed-Material Transport Equation Calculations

Application of the Parker (1990a, b) and Wilcock and Crowe (2003) bed-material transport equations for seven cross sections over 39 years indicates considerable spatial and temporal variability in predicted annual transport volumes (figs. 31 and 32). On the basis of the overall consistency in predicted transport capacity for the cross sections in the Upper and Emily Creek reaches (fig. 31) and the agreement between measured and predicted transport rates (fig. 30), we judge the results for the cross section at FPkm 15.3 to be representative of the volume of bed material entering the study reach. For this "reference" cross section (fig. 30C), predictions of bed-material influx into the reach range from less than 3,000 m^3/yr for some very dry years such as 1977 and 2001, to more than 150,000 m^3/yr for the wet years of 1982 and 1997 (fig. 32). The mean annual volume for the 1970–2008 period for this cross section is 51,100 m^3/yr as calculated by the Parker (1990 a, b) relation, and 73,900 m^3/yr based on the Wilcock and Crowe (2003) equation (table 6). These values are closely bracketed by 43,600–103,200 m^3/yr range encompassed by the predictions of mean annual transport for all four of the analyzed cross sections in the Upper and Emily Creek reaches.

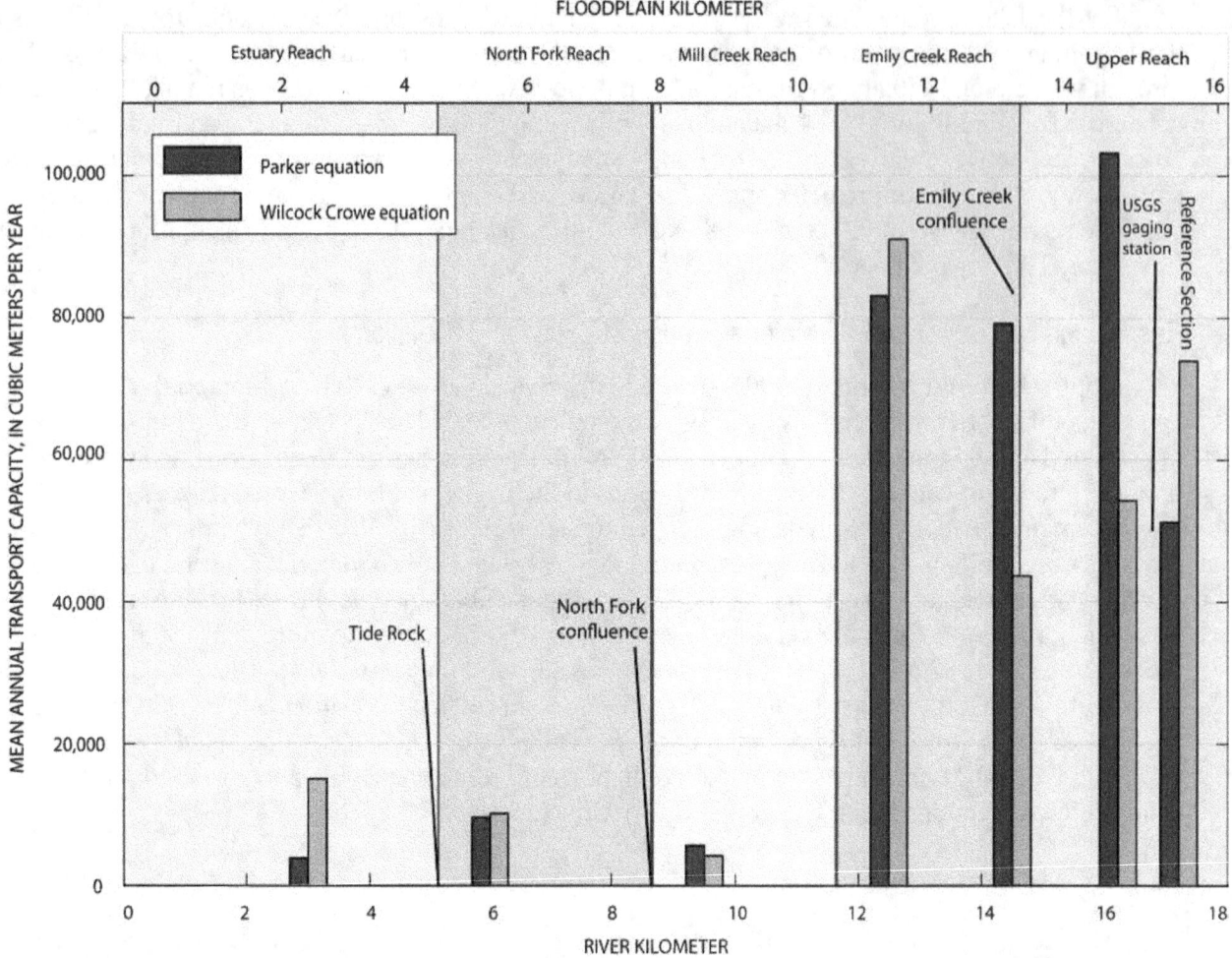

Figure 31. Graph showing mean annual predicted bed-material transport capacity for seven cross sections along the lower Chetco River, Oregon, for water years 1970–2008. Calculations based on Parker (1990, a, b) and Wilcock and Crowe (2003) transport equations. Hydraulics at each cross section from one-dimensional step-backwater hydraulic model for entire study reach.

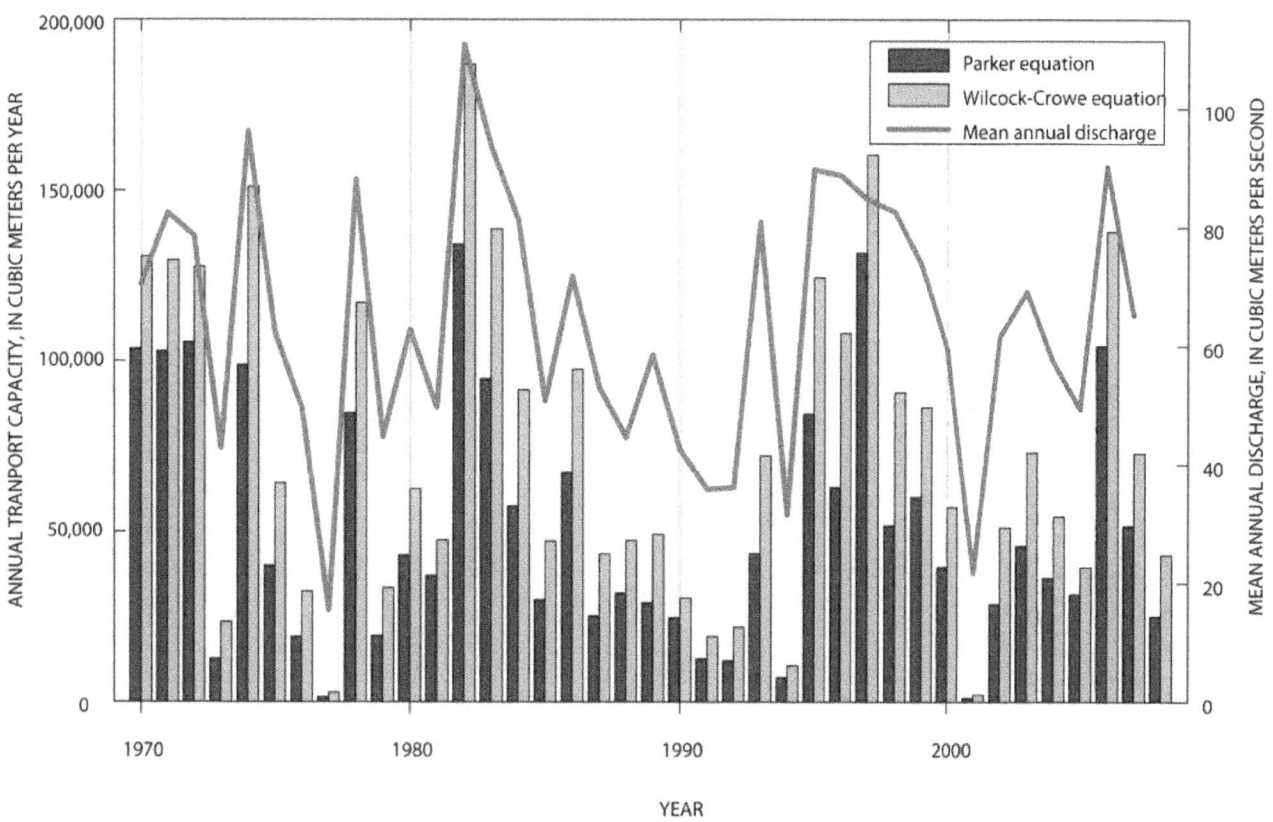

Figure 32. Graph showing mean annual discharge from USGS streamflow gaging station Chetco River near Brookings, Oregon (14400000). Annual bed-material transport capacity computed for reference cross section at floodplain kilometer 15.3 for water years 1970–2008 on basis of the Parker (1990 a, b) and Wilcock and Crowe (2003) transport relations.

For each of the seven analyzed cross sections, the predicted range of annual bed material transport averaged over the 39-year analysis period ranges from 3,900 m³/yr at FPkm 2.6 to 103,200 m³/yr at FPkm 14.9 for the Parker (1990 a, b) equation, and 4,100 m³/yr at FPkm 8.5 to 91,100 m³/yr at FPkm 11.5 for the Wilcock and Crowe (2003) equation (fig. 32). The section-to-section spatial variability of mean annual transport rates along the channel is probably not indicative of actual conditions because of (1) differences in the suitability of particular cross sections for bed-material transport calculations because of factors such as flow obstructions and along cross section variations in shear stress, (2) poor characterization of local surface particle size distributions, particularly since some analyzed cross sections were up to 850 m away from the nearest sediment sampling location, and (3) differences in the accuracy of the hydraulic modeling for each cross section, particularly in regards to calculated values of S_f, which is a critical flow parameter controlling transport rates (Wilcock and others, 2009). Nevertheless, the general trends evident in figure 32—transport capacities of 40,000 to 100,000 m³/yr in the Upper and Emily Creek Reaches, diminishing downstream to less than 10,000 m³/yr in the Mill Creek Reach—probably closely indicate overall transport conditions. As described subsequently, this pattern is also consistent with geomorphic evidence of historical sedimentation in the lower Mill Creek and North Fork reaches.

The annual variability in predicted bed-material transport capacity is also high (fig. 32), but this is attributable to the nonlinear relation between bed material transport and flow coupled with the high year-to-year flow variability. For the reference cross section at FPkm 15.3, the annual calculated bed-material volumes range from 1,067 m³/yr in the very dry year of 2001, as calculated by the Parker (1990 a, b) relation to 160,500 m³/yr in water year 1997, as calculated by the Wilcock and Crowe (2003) equation. The distribution of predicted annual transport volumes is negatively skewed, meaning that the majority of years—about 60 percent—have transport rates less than the mean value. The 2002 water year record highlights the temporal variability within a single year; for this year the total bed-material transport predicted by the Parker (1990 a, b) equation is 28,600 m³/s, but half of this volume is predicted to have been transported in a 6-day period encompassing less than 2 percent of the year (fig. 33).

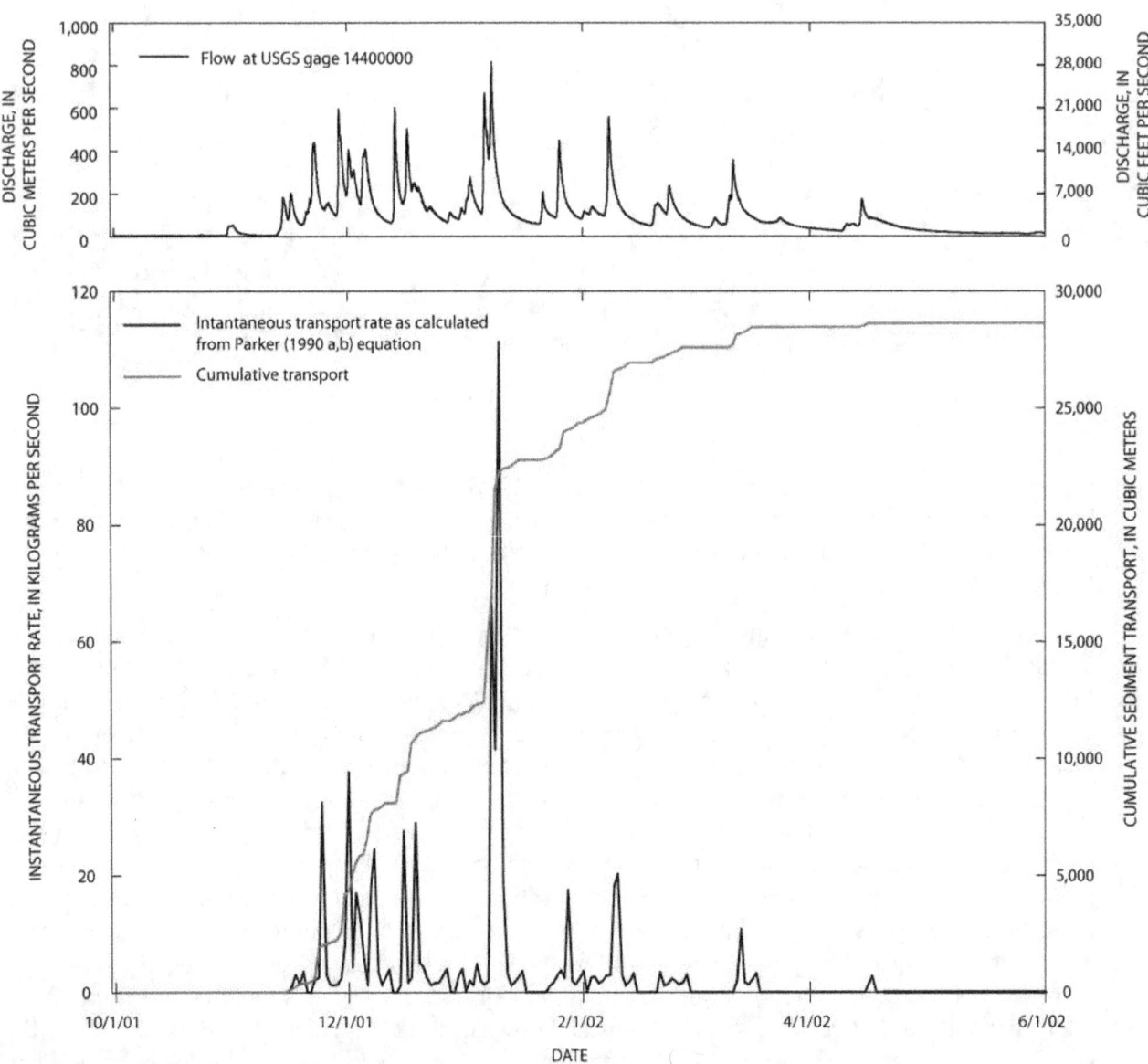

Figure 33. Graphs showing calculated bed-material transport for water year 2002 at reference cross section at floodplain kilometer 15.3, Chetco River, Oregon.

In general, the Parker (1990 a, b) and Wilcock and Crowe (2003) relations produce total annual volume estimates that agree to within a factor of 2 for most analyzed cross sections. Differences in predicted transport capacities between the two equations chiefly owe to the sand content of the surface bed material, with the Wilcock and Crowe (2003) relation predicting higher transport rates at cross sections where the sand content is higher, such as for the downstream-most site at FPkm 2.6. For cross sections where the surface samples had little sand, such as those at FPkm 11.5, 8.5, and 5.4, the equations agree to within 10 percent (table 6).

Quantitative assessment of the uncertainty of the transport values derived from application of these bed-material capacity equations is challenging, especially for situations of few actual measurements (Pitlick and others, 2009). The two direct bedload discharge measurements support selection of the Wilcock and Crowe (2003) and Parker (1990a, b) equations for calculating transport capacity, as well as the underlying assumption that bed-material transport is indeed a function of streamflow rather than supply. Measurements are lacking, however, to test these equations and assumptions for elsewhere in the study reach. Beyond uncertainty owing to the semiempirical nature of the equations, uncertainty and errors arise from channel geometry, flow and sediment texture characterizations. A range of these parameters are embodied, however, in calculated transport rates for each of the cross sections, and the resulting range of mean annual transport volume of 51,120–103,200 m^3/yr (as calculated by the Parker equation (1990 a, b)) for the four cross sections in the Upper and Emily Creek reaches transport relation provides an indication of the effects of such uncertainty owing to characterization of local conditions. Systematic analysis of the effects surface bed-material size on calculated transport rates for the reference cross section at FPkm 15.3 shows that a ± 10 percent variation in the surface grain size distribution results in 20–35 percent difference in predicted transport rates, indicating that transport capacity is highly sensitive to surface bed-sediment texture.

One independent check of the overall reasonableness of these predicted values is consideration of the predicted transport volumes relative to bar area. For water year 2005, the Parker (1990 a, b) and Wilcock and Crowe (2003) equations applied to the reference cross section predict 31,500 and 39,500 m^3 entering the study area, respectively, volumes that translate to seemingly reasonable values of 15–20 cm of deposition on all the bare bars (which generally correspond to the low elevation bar surfaces) as mapped in the study reach from aerial photographs taken in the summer of 2005.

The primary means by which uncertainty in the transport equations could be reduced is by more direct bedload measurements. Additional measurements would allow additional checking of the equations used in this analysis or enabling use of the calibrated transport equations of Bakke and others (1999) and Wilcock (2001). If a sufficient number of measurements were available over a wide range of flows, a site-specific empirical equation relating bed-material transport to flow could supplant the application of the equations and allow for more rigorous assessments of uncertainty.

Estimation of Bed-Material Flux by Assessment of Channel Change

An independent approach to assessing the transport rates of bed material is to exploit the intrinsic relation between rates of channel change in alluvial rivers and rates of sediment transport. This type of "morphology-based" based approach (Popov, 1962; Martin and Church, 1995) relates volumetric change within a reach to assumptions regarding storage, annual transport lengths, or independent boundary conditions to provide annual estimates of bed-material flux. Morphology-based approaches to estimating sediment budgets have been applied to numerous gravel-bed rivers throughout the world, including many rivers in similar environments as the Chetco River (Collins and Dunne, 1989; Martin and Church, 1995; McLean and Church, 1999; Ham and Church, 2000; Gaueman and others, 2003;

Martin and Ham, 2005; Surian and Cisotto, 2007). In proper settings, this approach has the advantage of (1) being based on actual measurements of observed channel change, (2) being potentially applied for multiple time periods and in the absence of flow data, and (3) integrating multiple transport events in determining bed-material fluxes, thereby avoiding the uncertainties in predicting transport from applying strongly nonlinear transport relations to highly variable flows.

Morphologic Analysis

Estimates of bed-material transport rates require volumetric estimates of changes in bed material for specific time periods. For the Chetco River, most bed material is stored in the bars flanking the low-flow channel, so this analysis focused on estimating changes in bar volume. Estimates of volumetric change are best acquired from repeat high-resolution topographic surveys (Martin and Church, 1995; McLean and Church, 1999) but in the absence of such surveys, they are commonly obtained by mapping planview changes between sequential sets of aerial photographs and estimating the thickness of bed material involved in the mapped changes (Collins and Dunne, 1989; Gaueman and others, 2003). Short analysis periods are preferable to reduce the negative bias in calculated volumetric change introduced by possible repeated erosion and deposition at the same location by multiple events. Consequently, the ideal situation is to calculate volumetric changes after each transporting flow (Lindsay and Ashmore, 2002), but the more typical circumstance is to rely upon aerial photograph sequences spanning periods of less than 5 years. A potentially favorable situation for future analyses made possible recently is the opportunity to accurately determine volumetric changes by repeat LIDAR surveys using the survey in 2008 as a starting point.

For the Chetco River study area, we applied this approach using sequences of aerial photographs and the LIDAR survey of 2008, which together span five time intervals: 1939–1943, 1962–1965, 1995–2000, 2000–2005, and 2005–2008. This analysis was based on the maps of the active channel areas described previously. For each time period, we overlaid the maps of active channel features to create three polygon classes (fig. 34): "Erosion," "Deposition" or "No Volumetric Change." Erosion polygons were assigned to areas where a bar or floodplain feature mapped on the first photograph set became a water feature on the second photograph set of the analysis pair. Likewise, "Deposition" polygons were those that changed from water to bar (in cases water became floodplain). Areas that did not change between land and water were classified as "No Volumetric Change."

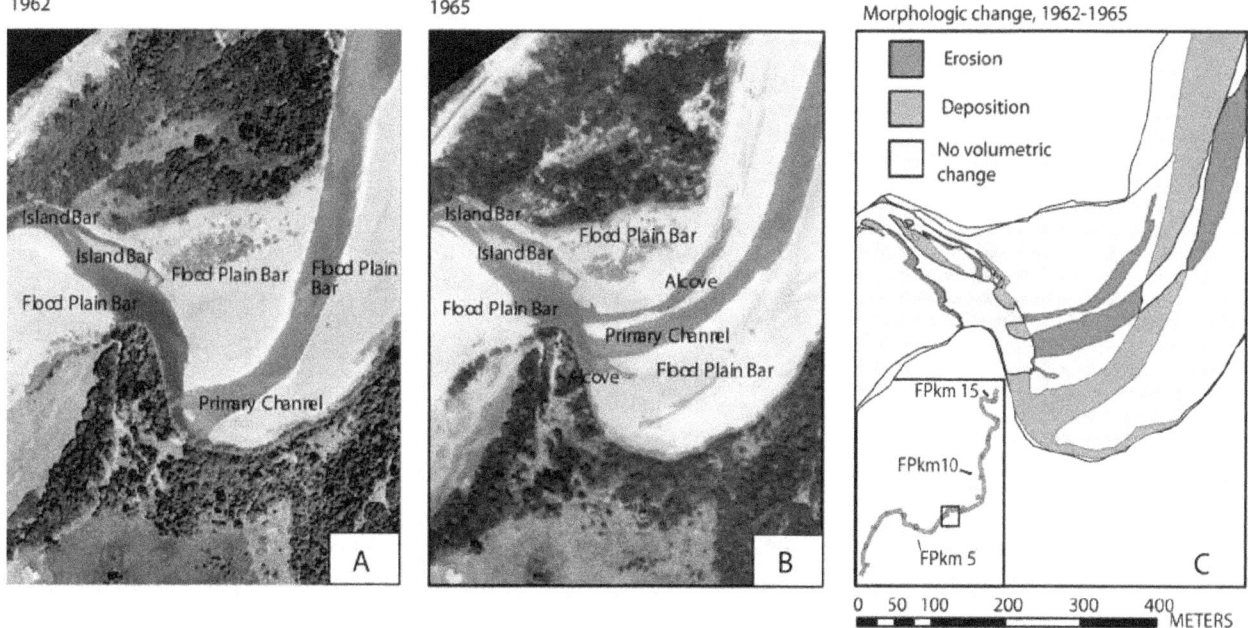

Figure 34. Maps showing example of erosion and deposition classification for morphologic analysis near floodplain kilometer 7, Chetco River, Oregon. A. 1962 Channel and bar mapping. B. 1965 Channel and bar mapping. C. 1962–65 erosion, deposition, and no-change classifications. FPkm, floodplain kilometer.

Because this approach relies on the accurate mapping of depositional and erosional areas, several steps were taken to reduce mapping errors and georeferencing and rectification uncertainties. These steps included reclassifying some features on the active-channel maps to avert erroneous designations and transitions, such as classifying small disconnected water bodies as "Deposition" because they were water filled on one photograph but dry on the next. We also eliminated all very small areas (mostly less than 10 m^2 but as large as 200 m^2) that possibly resulted from imprecise registration or digitization of features that had not seemingly changed. These areas, however, cumulatively represent only a very small percentage of the total depositional and erosional areas; for example, for the period between 1939 and 1943, the total area excluded by these uncertain polygons was less than 2 percent of total area of change. Each of the polygons remaining after this process was inspected at 1:3,000 to verify assigned classifications.

As for the assessment of temporal trends in bar area, different discharges (and stages) between photo sets in analysis pairs were accounted for by adjusting the net area of erosion or deposition by the estimated difference in bar area owing to the difference in discharge (fig. 7). For certain year pairs, such as 2005 and 2008, for which the difference in discharge is small, this adjustment is very small. But for analysis periods such as 1939–43 and 1995–2000, this adjustment is large relative to the area of net erosion or deposition (fig. 35, table 7).

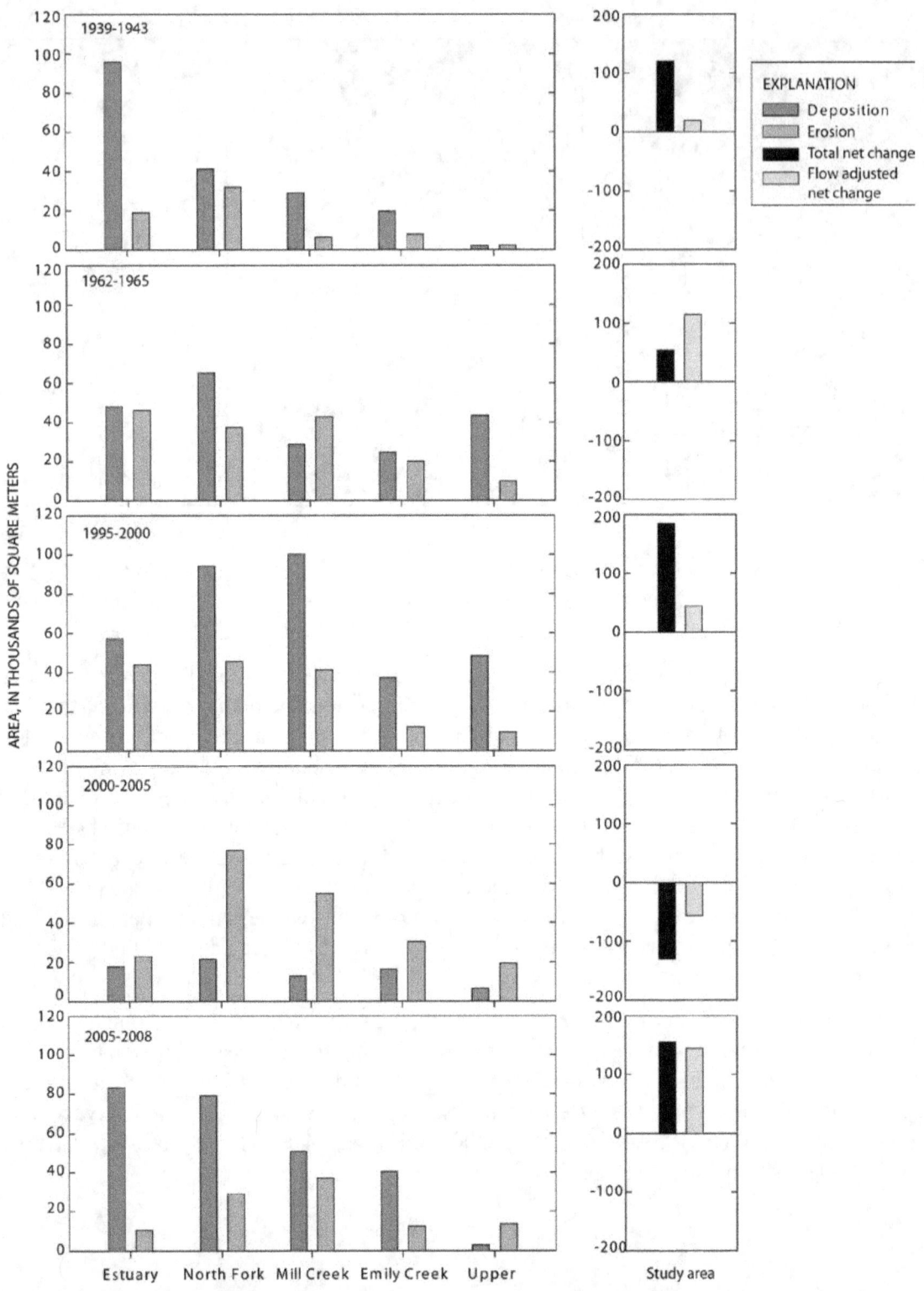

Figure 35. Graphs showing areas of bed-material erosion and deposition volumes for selected time periods in the Chetco River, Oregon. Individual reach measurements not adjusted for difference in flow stage. For each time period, however, the total net change for the study reach was adjusted for flow difference between photo sets (fig. 7) to determine "flow-adjusted net change" to use in calculating net bed-material influx to the study reach.

Table 7. Summary of morphology-based sediment-transport-volume estimates for the Chetco River, Oregon

[Abbreviations: m^2, square meters; m^3, cubic meters; --, no data]

	Period				
	1939–1943	1962–1965	1995–2000	2000–2005	2005–2008
Period length (years)	4	3	5	5	3
Area of eroded bar (m^2)	67,000	157,000	152,000	204,000	102,000
New bar area (m^2)	187,000	211,000	337,000	74,000	257,000
Net measured change in bar area (m^2)	120,000	54,000	185,000	-130,000	155,000
Flow-adjusted change in bar area (m^2)	19,000	115,000	44,000	-57,000	144,000
Scenario 1: Erosion and deposition, where bar height in each reach is average of all bars					
Volume of erosion (m^3)	183,000	443,000	421,000	560,000	283,000
Volume of deposition (m^3)	538,000	598,000	942,000	214,000	723,000
Net change in bed material (m^3)	355,000	155,000	521,000	-346,000	440,000
Flow-adjusted net change in bed material (m^3)	42,000	333,000	100,000	-150,000	411,000
Annual net balance [3] (m^3/yr)	89,000	52,000	104,000	-69,000	147,000
Flow-adjusted annual net balance [3] (m^3/yr)	11,000	111,000	25,000	-30,000	137,000
Scenario 2: Erosion and deposition, where bar height in each reach is average of all low bars					
Volume of erosion (m^3)	116,000	282,000	268,000	338,000	171,000
Volume of deposition (m^3)	361,000	375,000	581,000	133,000	462,000
Net change in bed material (m^3)	245,000	93,000	313,000	-205,000	291,000
Flow-adjusted net change in bed material (m^3)	56,000	204,000	75,000	-85,000	273,000
Annual net balance [3] (m^3/yr)	61,000	31,000	63,000	-41,000	97,000
Flow-adjusted annual net balance [3] (m^3/yr)	14,000	68,000	15,000	-17,000	91,000
Scenario 3: Erosion calculated using reach average height of all bars; Deposition calculated using reach average height of low bars					
Volume erosion	183,000	443,000	421,000	560,000	283,000
Volume of deposition	361,000	375,000	581,000	133,000	462,000
Net change in bed material (m^3)	178,000	-68,000	160,000	-427,000	179,000
Flow-adjusted net change in bed material (m^3)	-48,000	81,000	-145,000	-245,000	153,000
Annual net balance [3] (m^3/yr)	44,000	-22,000	32,000	-85,000	59,000
Flow-adjusted annual net balance[3] (m^3/yr)	-12,000	27,000	-29,000	-49,000	51,000
Summary Ranges: Flow-adjusted annual net balances (m^3)	-12,000 to 14,000	-27,000 to 111,000	-29,000 to 25,000	-49,000 to -17,000	51,000 to 137,000

Table 7. Summary of morphology-based sediment-transport-volume estimates for the Chetco River, Oregon—continued

[Abbreviations: m^2, square meters; m^3, cubic meters; --, no data]

	Period				
	1939–1943	1962–1965	1995–2000	2000–2005	2005–2008
Summary Comparisons					
Total volume (m³) removed due to gravel mining[1]	--	--	160,000	310,000	185,000
Total bed-material (m³) influx as predicted by transport equations[2]	--	--	390,000 to 530,000	190,000 to 270,000	200,000 to 270,000
Total bed-material (m³) influx as predicted by morphologic approach (flow-adjusted) and accounting for gravel extraction volumes[4]	--	--	15,000 to 260,000	65,000 to 225,000	338,000 to 596,000
Average annual lower Chetco River influx from bedload transport equations [5](m³/yr)	--	--	78,000 to 106,000	38,000 to 54,000	67,000 to 90,000
Annual lower Chetco River bed-material influx as calculated from range of flow-adjusted morphologic estimates and accounting for gravel extraction volumes, and assuming no bed-material transport out the lower river (m³/yr)	[6]-12,000 to 14,000	[6]-27,000 to 111,000	3,000 to 52,000	13,000 to 45,000	113,000 to 197,000

[1] Gravel mining volumes were provided by operators (fig. 6), and in some cases are estimated. Total volume of extraction for each period only includes extraction bracketed by the dates of the photographs used in the mapping; for example, the mined volume for 1995–2000 includes extraction from 1995, 1996, 1997, and 1999

[2] The sediment influx was calculated using the equations of Wilcock and Crowe (2003) and Parker (1990 a, b). Totals reported here assume no sediment transport the latter part of the water year (July-September) and were calculated by summing transport for each of the water years bracketed by the mapping periods. For example, the sediment load for 1995-2000 includes transport from the 1996, 1997, 1998, 1999, and 2000 water years, but assumes no transport for the latter part of 1995 post-dating the May 27 date of the 1995 aerial photographs.

[3] The annualized net balance was computed by dividing the difference between deposition and erosion by the number of years in the period.

[4] The ranges reflect all three bar-thickness scenarios

[5] Annual fluxes calculated by dividing period totals by the number of years in the analysis period; range encompasses different predictions by the Wilcock and Crowe (2002) and Parker (1990 a, b) equations for each period.

[6] Assumes negligable gravel extraction, therefore probably underestimates true influx values.

More difficult to infer from the aerial photograph pairs is the thickness of bed material involved in areas of erosion and deposition, a critical parameter for estimating volumes. The approach used was to designate characteristic bar thicknesses for each reach, which were then multiplied by erosional and depositional areas to obtain corresponding volumes. An upper limit for characteristic bar thickness was determined from measurements of average bar elevation above the channel thalweg, measured by GIS analysis of the channel and LIDAR topographic measurements for 543 orthogonals spaced at 30-m intervals along the channel centerline and stratified by reach (fig. 36). Calculated in this manner, average bar height in 2008 ranged from 2.4 m in the North Fork Reach to 3.7 m for the Emily Creek Reach.

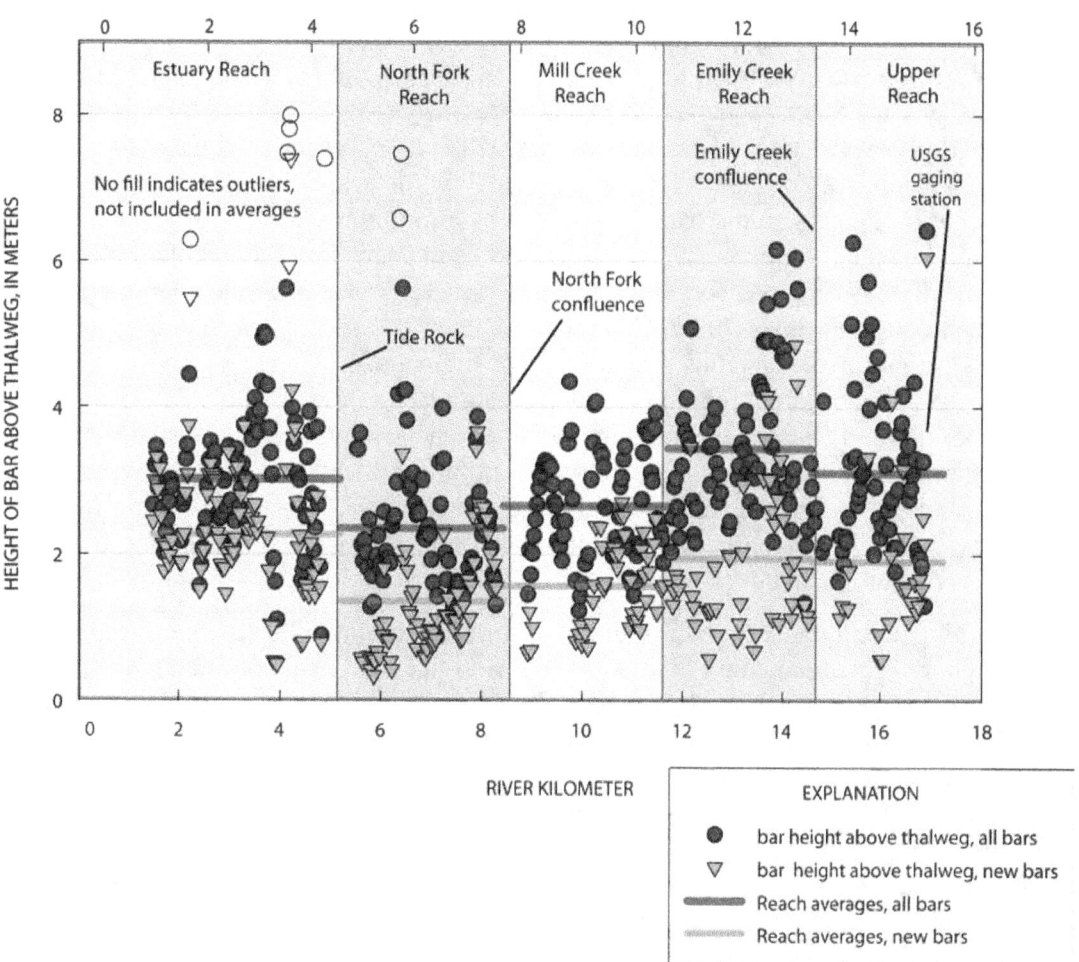

Figure 36. Graph showing bar thickness values used to calculate erosion and deposition volumes from changes in bar area in the Chetco River, Oregon. Values determined by difference of average bar elevation and thalweg elevation at 30-m intervals along the floodplain centerline, and averaged for each reach. "All bars" include all bars mapped from 2008 LIDAR. "New bars" are bars that formed between 2005 and 2008, are typically lower, and are inferred to more closely represent the thickness of new deposits.

To determine a lower bound, and one that probably better reflects deposit thickness for newly formed bars, we used the same analysis but evaluated elevations only from bars created between 2005 and 2008 (fig. 36), resulting in estimates of "new bar" average thicknesses between 1.5 and 2.3 m (relative to thalweg) depending on reach. Implicit in using these new-bar values for earlier analysis periods is that the relation between channel thalweg elevation and bar height is similar for all time periods. As we have shown from the channel change analysis, however, this assumption is probably not valid for certain periods, and the channel lowering since the late 1970s (without substantial coincident bar lowering) may result in volume overestimates for earlier time periods, especially for the periods 1939–43 and 1962–65, which predate channel incision. Also difficult to infer from aerial photographs is the thickness of deposition or scour on surfaces not changing status during an observation period, including gravel bars and areas within the low-flow channel. These volumes are not considered by our analysis, but could be evaluated in future analyses with additional LIDAR or high resolution topographic surveys.

Assessment of Sediment Volumes from Morphologic Analysis

On the basis of three depositional and erosional thickness scenarios, we calculated areas and volumes of erosion and deposition for each of the five time periods and for each of the five reaches, using three scenarios for erosional and depositional thickness (fig. 35, table 7). The three scenarios involved multiplying the areas of erosion and deposition by (1) reach-average values for average bar thickness, (2) reach-average values for average new-bar thickness, and (3) what we judge as the most realistic scenario of calculating erosional volumes by multiplying the area of erosion by the average thickness of all bars but using the average thickness of the new bars for calculating depositional volumes. This latter scenario is certainly most appropriate for the 2005–08 analysis period, because the value for the average thickness of new bars was obtained specifically for this time period. Evident from this analysis is that for all scenarios, measured deposition and erosion areas and volumes as determined from changes in bar area are larger in the downstream reaches (fig 35, table 7). Also evident is that for most time periods and reaches, this measurement approach shows more deposition than erosion. The periods of greatest positive net change, after accounting for differences in flow, were the 1962–65 and 2005–08 periods, both spanning exceptional floods. The relatively dry 2000–05 period is the only one for which every reach apparently lost bed-material volume, even after accounting for the higher flow on the 2005 aerial photographs.

Estimating actual transport rates requires additional assumptions. The simplest situation and the one applied here is to assume no gravel transport from the river to the ocean, and to consider the net changes to represent bed-material influx rates for the entire lower Chetco River. This approach has been applied to several of the British Columbia studies, in which bed material fines downstream and the channels transition from gravel to sand bed (Martin and Church, 1995; McLean and Church, 1999; Ham and Church, 2000). This assumption may not apply perfectly here because of the historical presence of isolated gravel bars downstream to FPkm 1. Nevertheless, the few bars in the lower 3 km, the downstream reduction in bed-material grain size (fig. 22), and the 80- to 90–percent decrease in transport capacity (fig. 31) predicted by the transport equations for conditions in 2008 indicate that the flux of gravel-size bed material exiting the study reach is a very small fraction of that coming in. Accordingly, the net volume accumulated in the study reach is a minimum indication of bed-material flux at the upstream end of the study reach. A more complete assessment includes the volume removed by gravel extraction (Martin and Church, 1995), thereby implicitly assuming that the mining volumes have been replenished without significantly affecting bar and channel boundaries. This assumption is approximately correct for the Chetco River where recent gravel extraction has been by bar skimming at locations away from the low channel, and that repeat surveys show substantial replenishment most years (Ted Freeman, Freeman Rock Inc. and Robert Elayer, Tidewater Contractors Inc., written commun., 2008). Therefore, for the summary calculation of lower Chetco River bed-material influx from the morphologic approach, we have added the reported volumes of mined gravel for the 1995–2000, 2000–05, and 2005–08 periods (table 7).

Total volumetric changes and flux estimates are best assessed for the more recent periods for which thickness estimates are most valid and for when we have the most reliable estimates of the volume of gravel extracted by mining. For the period 2005–08, the total calculated net volume change ranges from 179,000 to 440,000 m^3 for the three thickness scenarios (table 7). The low end of this range is from our preferred scenario of using average thickness of all bars to calculate erosional volumes but only the thickness of new bars to determine depositional volumes, and gives an annual net volume of 59,000 m^3/yr. Adjusting this value for the difference in discharge in the source imagery for the 2005 and 2008 mapping lowers the average bed-material sediment balance to about 51,000 m^3/yr. Accounting for the 62,000 m^3/yr removed by gravel mining during 2005–07 (the LIDAR of 2008 was acquired before that year's gravel mining) results in an estimated total gravel influx into the lower Chetco River of 113,000 m^3/yr for the 2005–8 analysis period. This value is probably best considered a minimum value as a consequence of (1) the negative biases inherent in the method, especially for periods spanning multiple transport events (Martin and Church, 1995), (2) the assumption that little bed material leaves the river, and (3) our choice of a thickness scenario that minimizes positive volumes; although incomplete replenishment of mined areas would bias this value positively. Similar calculations for the other two analysis periods with gravel extraction data indicate annual bed-material influxes ranging from 3,000 m^3/yr during 1995–2000 to the 32,000 m^3/yr measured for 2000–05. For the earlier periods for which there is no reliable gravel extraction information, annual influx rates considering only the changes in bar area are small for 1939–43 (-12,000 to 14,000 m^3/yr) and possibly large for 1962–65 (-27,000 to 111,000 m^3/yr), but the wide range resulting from the various thickness scenarios and the undetermined volume of removed gravel makes these values highly uncertain.

The high influx values for 2005–08 compared to the lower values calculated for the period 2000–05 correspond with overall high and low flow for those periods (fig. 2). In addition, the values of annual influx, considering the range of thickness scenarios, correspond within a factor of 3 to those predicted by the bedload transport equations for these two time periods. For the period 1995–2000, however, the morphologic method predicts substantially smaller influxes than the transport equations.

The spatial variations in areas of erosion and deposition are consistent with the overall geomorphology (fig. 35). The Upper Reach has had only small net changes in sediment accumulation volumes, and this narrow section apparently has little dynamic storage. We infer that the gravel bars within this reach have morphologies in approximate equilibrium between deposition and erosion, with entrainment approximately balanced by deposition during each transporting flow. More dynamic storage has been accommodated by the wider and lower gradient reaches downstream, particularly the Mill Creek, North Fork, and Estuary Reaches. For the Estuary Reach in particular, the analysis periods have been ones of bar growth, although this is counter to the overall trend for this reach during the entire historical period (figs. 9 and 10).

Although this method as applied here shows the main areas of deposition and offers broad constraints on deposition and erosional volumes which can in turn provide estimates of total bed-material influxes, the multiple assumptions and uncertainties reduce precision and accuracy. The main factors hindering robust estimates are (1) the multiple year periods between photograph sets, (2) relying upon planview changes to estimate volumetric changes and the resulting uncertainty due to poor knowledge of the thickness of eroded and deposited areas, and (3) the substantial effects of flow stage in determining areas of erosion and deposition. For the Chetco River, these issues could be overcome by a sustained program of repeated high-resolution topographic and bathymetric surveys. Much more accurate morphometric estimates of sediment accumulation and erosion could be made from such surveys, for which the LIDAR of 2008 could serve as high-quality starting point.

Bed-Material Sediment Budget for the Lower Chetco River

Consideration of all these bed-material analyses allows for an approximate sediment budget broadly consistent with many of the study observations (fig. 37). As calculated from the transport capacity equations, the average bed-material influx into the upstream end of the study reach for the 39-year period of 1970–2008 was probably in the range of 40,000–100,000 m^3/yr. Approximately 5–30 percent of this influx is probably lost to particle attrition and breakdown, and is carried to the Pacific Ocean or overbank areas by suspended load transport. The volume lost to bed-material attrition is approximately balanced by bed material supplied by tributaries to the lower Chetco River. The transport capacity calculations, channel mapping, and morphologic analyses indicate that the majority of the bed-material influx has been accumulating in depositional areas within the Mill Creek, North Fork, and Estuary reaches, with perhaps little bed-material sediment exiting the lower river. Net deposition in these reaches approximately matches or slightly exceeds the 59,000 m^3/yr extracted for aggregate during 2000–2008, but was almost certainly exceeded by the 1976–1980 rate of 140,000 m^3/yr (Marquess and Associates, 1980). The substantial downstream fining and transport capacity equations indicate that most bed material is likely retained in the lower Chetco River, with little transport, especially of gravel, to the Pacific Ocean.

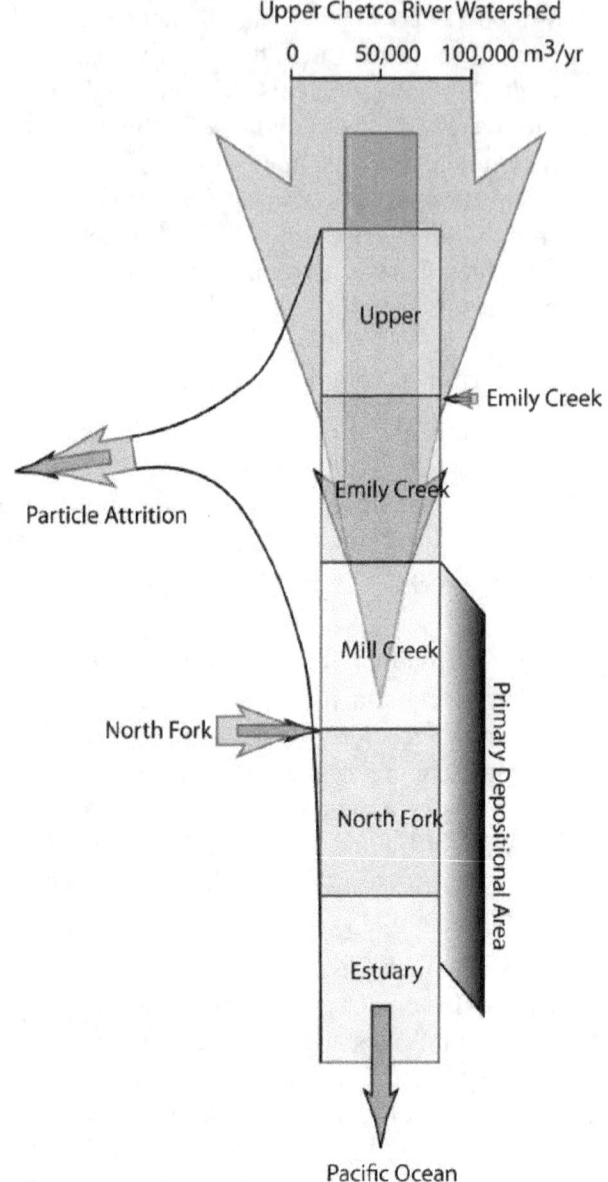

Figure 37. Schematic diagram of sediment budget for the lower Chetco River, Oregon. Arrow widths are proportional to annual flux; ranges indicate estimated uncertainty.

Comparison with Sediment Yield from Regional Drainage Basins

Although there has been little previous work on Chetco River sediment transport, geologic analyses and studies of other watersheds allow comparisons and an evaluation of the reasonableness of the results obtained here. This study focused on the key question of bed-material influx into the study reach because this is a central issue to understanding overall sediment conditions. From a wide range of considerations, including geologic uplift rates, hillslope sediment production, and actual bed-material measurement programs, estimates for bed-material production range from 26 to 610 $m^3/km^2/yr$ for several northern California and southern Oregon coastal drainage basins, with most values being between 40 and 180 $m^3/km^2/yr$ (table 8). This range translates to 28,000–126,000 m^3/yr for the 703 km^2 contributing area at the upstream end of the Chetco River study reach, encompassing the 40,000–100,000 m^3/yr predicted by the transport capacity equations and many of the period influx rates indicated by the morphologic analyses (table 7).

Table 8. Estimates of bedload production rates for northern California and southern Oregon coastal drainage basins

[**Abbreviations:** USEPA, U.S. Environmental Protection Agency; USGS, U.S. Geological Survey; m, meter; km, kilometer; yr, year. Where applicable, bedload was assumed to be 20 percent of total load. Sediment production rates for this study were scaled to the contributing area at USGS streamflow gage 14400000, 702 km^2.]

Source	Area of study	Period described	Method	Bedload production rates, m^3/km^2-yr^1
Kelsey and Bockheim, 1994	Southern Oregon Coast, including Chetco Bay	Holocene	Uplift rate, assuming equilibrium	140–180
E.G. Andrews, U.S. Geological Survey, written commun., 2008	Northern California Rivers	1950–2006	Bedload equation	26-610
USEPA, 1999	Van Duzen River, California	1955–1999	Landslide volume analysis, field mapping	80–100
Raines and Kelsey, 1991	Grouse Creek, California	1960–1989	Landslide volume analysis	130
Russell, 1994	Pistol River, Oregon	1940–1991	Landslide volume analysis	80–110
MFG Inc. and others, 2006	Smith River, Oregon	1932–2003	Calibrated bedload equation	40

Summary of Bed-Material Observations and Analyses

These analyses of bed material, transport measurements and calculations, and deposition and erosion patterns support the following observations and conclusions regarding sediment in the Chetco River:

The geologic and geomorphic environment of the lower Chetco River is of long-term bed-material accumulation in response to Holocene sea level rise. The present locus of sedimentation (and consequent channel dynamism) is in the area of the North Fork confluence. Recent and ongoing uplift in conjunction with active hillslope erosion processes supply abundant coarse detritus to the channel from much of the drainage basin.

The alluvial valley bottom, bed-sediment textures, armoring ratios, and close agreement between transport relations for bed-material transport indicate a balance between sediment supply and transport capacity at the upstream end of the study reach. Hence, Chetco River bed-material transport into the lower Chetco River is probably limited by transport capacity, rather than sediment supply.

Applying established transport equations for multiple cross sections at the upstream end of the reach gives likely mean annual bed-material transport rates into the lower Chetco River of approximately 40,000–100,000 m^3/yr for water years 1970–2008, with the reference cross section at the upstream end of the study reach giving a narrower range of 51,100–73,900 m^3/yr (fig. 31). On a per unit area, the influx values for the Chetco River are similar to those from nearby coastal drainage basins (table 8). Because of year-to-year flow variability, predicted influx of bed-material ranges from less than 3,000 m^3 in dry years to over 150,000 m^3 for wet years with large floods such as 1982 and 1997 (fig. 32).

Transport capacity, as predicted by the transport equations, diminishes substantially downstream, from values approaching the influx rates in the Upper and Emily Creek reaches to less than 10,000 m^3/yr for the North Fork and Estuary reaches (fig. 32). The decreased transport capacity of these downstream reaches is consistent with these reaches being long-term areas of sedimentation as indicated by active channel migration and bar deposition (figs. 13 and 14).

The morphologic approach to estimating bed-material influx into the study reach gives a much wider range of results, with annual reach-scale net volume changes ranging up to 200,000 m^3/yr for the 2005–8 period. For this period, this rate of bed-sediment influx is about twice that predicted by the transport relation equations. For the other two time periods when the methods can be compared, the morphologic approach gives influx rates equivalent, or less than, that predicted by the bed-material transport relations (table 7). The assumptions and uncertainties intrinsic to the morphologic approach when when based on historical aerial photographs reduce the utility of the morphologic analyses as applied for the Chetco River. But this approach could be valuable and much more accurate if based on annually collected high-resolution topographic data.

Bed material input from tributaries is approximately balanced by loss of volume by particle breakage and attrition.

The predicted downstream decrease in transport capacity, the small bed-sediment particle sizes in the downstream bars, and the rough congruence between the net volume changes determined from the morphologic method with the predicted sediment influx into the reach indicate that, in the absence of gravel extraction, most bed-material sediment entering into the lower Chetco River remains in the study reach, with most probably stored in the Mill Creek, North Fork, and Estuary Reaches.

The downstream increase in armoring and surface coarsening (fig. 22) may indicate that sediment supply in the North Fork and Estuary Reaches is less than flow capacity.

The best estimates of mean annual bed material influx from this study—40,000–100,000 m^3/yr— are of similar magnitude or slightly exceed the volume of gravel mined for the 1993–2008 period (fig. 6). For low flow years such as 2001, gravel extraction almost certainly exceeded supply. For high-flow years such as 2006, bed-material influx likely exceeded the volume mined. The voluminous gravel mining in the late 1970s (Marquess and Associates, 1980) probably exceeded replenishment rates by at least a factor of 3.

Summary

Our analysis of the lower 16 km of the gravel-bed Chetco River and its floodplain focused on understanding bed-material transport and its relation to channel and floodplain morphology. The main study components were (1) detailed mapping and surveying of the valley bottom to document spatial and temporal changes to the channel and flanking bars and floodplains and (2) quantitative investigation of the flux of bed material into and through the study reach. These study components have resulted in a mutually consistent and coherent understanding of the recent history of the active channel and how observed changes may relate to the influx and removal of bed sediment.

Primary Findings

The Chetco River is a wandering gravel-bed river flanked by abundant and large gravel bars formed of coarse bed-material sediment. The upper reaches of the study area are primarily transport zones, with bar positions fixed by valley geometry and the active bars mainly providing transient storage of bed material. The lower river has been aggrading in response to Holocene sea level rise. The Mill Creek and North Fork Reaches, between floodplain kilometer (FPkm) 5 and 10, have historically been the primary loci of this aggradation, with consequent active sedimentation and channel migration. Sediment transport capacity is limited in this reach and most net sediment influx into the study area probably accumulates here. A small amount of fine gravel is transported into the Estuary Reach. It is plausible that little gravel-sized bed sediment naturally exits the Chetco River.

The repeat surveys and map analyses indicate an overall reduction in bar area and local decreases in sinuosity, mainly between 1965 and 1995. Some loss of bar area owes to erosion and some has resulted from vegetation colonization and transition to vegetated and developed floodplain surfaces. Repeat topographic and bathymetric surveys indicate channel incision for significant portions of the study reach, with local values as high as 2 m. The specific gage analysis at the upstream end of the study reach indicates that recent incision may have followed aggradation culminating in the late 1970s. These observations are consistent with a reduction of sediment supply relative to transport capacity since at least the 1977 channel surveys. Also consistent with this is the trend of bed coarsening between FPkm 15.3 and FPkm 7.7 and the greater degree of armoring for the bars at FPkm 6 and 3 compared to a measurement at the upstream end of the reach.

Multiple and independent analyses, bolstered by direct measurements of bedload during winter 2008–09, indicate that the mean annual flux of bed material into the study reach is approximately 40,000–100,000 m^3/yr since 1970. The year-to-year flux, however, varies tremendously, with some years probably having little or no bed material entering the study reach, but for some high-flow years, such as 1982 and 1997, as much as 190,000 m^3/yr enters the reach. For comparison, the estimated annual volume of gravel extracted from the lower Chetco River for commercial aggregate has ranged from 5,000 to 90,000 m^3 and averaged about 59,000 m^3/yr between 2000 and 2008. Mined volumes, however, probably exceeded 140,000 m^3/yr for several years in the late 1970s, greatly surpassing likely replenishment rates.

The historical planform and vertical changes to the lower Chetco River, which almost certainly owe to a reduced sediment supply relative to transport capacity, have likely resulted from a combination of (1) bed-sediment removal and (2) transient effects as the river has adjusted to the probably large volume of sediment brought in by the 1964 flood. Fully disentangling these factors is not possible with existing information.

Implications Regarding Possible Future Trends and Monitoring Strategies

For a gravel-bed river such as the lower Chetco River, the physical character of the active channel is chiefly the result of bed-material transport processes. At the broad scale, the balance between bed-material transport capacity and sediment supply controls channel morphology. Details of channel conditions depend, however, on a variety of factors including the history of flow and sediment transport, the time lags involved in eroding and depositing sediment, and other local and drainage-basin-scale disturbances that might directly or indirectly affect the channel.

Despite these complexities, it is almost certain that if gravel removal exceeds bed-material influx, decreased bar areas and channel incision will ensue, similar to that of the late 1970s and 1980s. Such changes will likely be in conjunction with bed coarsening and possibly greater armoring of bar surfaces. Another probable outcome of a sediment deficit would be reduced migration rates, since bar deposition is a major cause of channel migration. Without gravel extraction, aggradation and enhanced channel migration is probable, probably first in the historical sedimentation area of the Mill Creek and North Fork Reaches. Because of the low transport capacity in these middle reaches, effects of enhanced sediment supply would probably take longer to affect the Estuary Reach. The time scales of changes depend foremost on sediment influx. A large influx associated with a flood like the one in 1964 could reverse most historical changes during the event. In contrast, the effects of sustained periods of excess transport capacity relative to sediment influx are likely to be manifest over years and decades, and possibly at diminishing rates as the channel and bars coarsen.

Because the sediment balance is a controlling factor, a key aspect of understanding possible effects of various management scenarios on the lower Chetco River is accurate knowledge of the volume of the influx of bed material. For the Chetco River, the bed-material capacity equations applied to the flow record provide seemingly reasonable estimates of bed-material influx to the lower river. This situation offers the opportunity, as long as there is continuous streamflow measurement, to provide annual (or even higher resolution) predictions of the volume of bed-material influx that could be used to guide management actions. Such analyses would be enhanced by a sustained bed-material measurement program, ideally involving at least one or two bedload transport measurements per year, to evaluate the reliability of the transport equations and ultimately develop a site specific bedload transport rating curve.

Another key for improving predictions of channel conditions and documenting effects of management actions is understanding the fate and effects of bed material sediment entering the reach. Repeat high-resolution topographic and bathymetric surveys of the entire active channel will (1) document the rates at which sediment is moving through the system, (2) allow identification of trends in vertical and planform channel behavior, and (3) provide independent assessment of the sediment influx and transport. Such surveys would ideally be supplemented by periodic bed-material sediment sampling for evaluating bed texture trends. Besides providing for direct and systematic monitoring of the active channel and enhancing understanding of key transport processes, this knowledge may be important for determining relevant management timescales by providing information on how long it may take the effects of management actions to have desired or detectable outcomes. In contrast, reach-scale interrelationships between sediment supply and channel and floodplain characteristics limit the utility of site-specific surveys for predicting and monitoring conditions in a manner responsive to typical management requirements.

From these considerations, an efficient and credible monitoring program would mainly focus on systemwide assessments of sediment influx and channel change. Sediment influx would probably be most reliably evaluated by annual analysis of the streamflow record, ideally supplemented by continued bedload transport measurements in order to improve the accuracy of the influx predictions and to confirm that the capacity-based equations remain appropriate. Continued channel-change assessments could be efficiently based on the LIDAR and estuary and channel surveys from 2008. Repeat high-resolution surveys at 1-year intervals would enable an independent check of the influx estimates as well as allow monitoring of trends in channel and floodplain conditions. These types of surveys could replace the site specific surveys with little or no loss of information relevant to trend monitoring. Even at lesser intervals, such surveys would probably provide trends and data useful for evaluating planform and vertical changes in the active channel. Monitoring of bed-sediment texture and vegetation could be less frequent (for example, 5–10 years) and would allow evaluation of how these important habitat attributes are changing with overall channel condition.

Acknowledgments

This study was guided by the State of Oregon Technical Team for instream gravel mining, chaired by Judy Linton of the Portland District of the U.S. Army Corps of Engineers, and including representatives from Oregon Department of State Lands, National Oceanic and Atmospheric Administration Fisheries, U.S. Fish and Wildlife Service, Oregon Department of Fish and Wildlife, Oregon Department of Environmental Quality, Oregon Coastal Management Program, and area gravel-mining companies. Surveying and bedload measurements were provided by the Central Point Field Office of the USGS Oregon Water Science Center under the leadership of Marc Stewart with guidance and analysis from Richard Kittelson and Roy Wellman of the Portland Field Office. John Risley of the USGS Oregon Water Science Center assisted with extending the streamflow record and Michelle Adams assisted with field measurements. Information on past gravel mining and access to measurement sites were provided by Tidewater Contractors Inc., South Coast Lumber Inc., and Freeman Rock Inc.; in particular Ted Freeman, Robert Elayer, Bill Yocum, Fred Arnold and Virgil Frazer were supportive. Ian Madin of the Oregon Department of Geology and Mineral Resources expedited transfer of LIDAR topography for our use. Bedload transport modeling was facilitated by provision of and assistance with the Bedload Assessment for Gravel-bed Streams (BAGS) software by John Pitlick, Yantao Cui, and Peter Wilcock. Robyn Darbyshire, U.S. Forest Service provided assistance with vegetation identification.

References Cited

American Society of Civil Engineers, 1999, Topographic surveying–Technical engineering and design guides as adapted from the U.S. Army Corps of Engineers, no. 29: American Society of Civil Engineers, 95 p.

Bakke, P.D., Basdekas, P.O., Dawdy, D.R., and Klingeman, P.C., 1999, Calibrated Parker-Klingeman model for gravel transport: Journal of Hydraulic Engineering, v. 125, p. 657–660.

Bowling, L.C., Storck, P., and Lettenmaier, D.P., 2000, Hydrologic effects of logging in Western Washington, United States: Water Resources Research, v. 36, no. 11, p. 3223–3240.

Buffington, J.M., and Montgomery, D.R., 1999, Effects of sediment supply on surface textures of gravel-bed rivers: Water Resources Research, v. 35, no. 11, p. 3523–3530.

Bunte, K. and Abt, S.R., 2001, Sampling surface and subsurface particle-size distributions in wadable grave- and cobble-bed streams for analyses in sediment transport, hydraulics, and stream-bed monitoring: U.S. Department of Agriculture, Forest Service, Rocky Mountain Research Station, General Technical Report RMRS-GTR-74, 428 p.

Burgette, R.J., Weldon II, R.J., and Schmidt, D.A., 2009, Interseismic uplift rates for western Oregon and along-strike variation in locking on the Cascadia subduction zone: Journal of Geophysical Research, v. 114, p. B01408. doi:10.1029/2008JB005679.

Chetco Watershed Council, 1995, Chetco River assessment: Chetco Watershed Council, 28 p.

Childers, D., 1992, Field comparison of four pressure-difference bedload samplers in high-energy flows: U.S. Geological Survey Water-Resources Investigations Report 92–4068, 59 p.

Church, M., 1983, Pattern of instability in a wandering gravel bed channel, *in* Collinson, J.D. and Lewis, J., eds., Modern and ancient fluvial systems: International Association of Sedimentologists Special Publication 6, p. 169–180.

Church, M., 1988, Floods in cold climates, *in* Baker, V.R., Kochel, R.C., and Patton, P.C., eds., Flood geomorphology: New York, John Wiley and Sons, p. 205–229.

Church, M., McLean, D.G., and Wolcott, D.F., 1987, River bed gravels: sampling and analysis, *in* Thorne, C.R., Bathurst, J.C., and Hey, R.D., eds., Sediment transport in gravel-bed rivers: Chichester, John Wiley and Sons, p. 43–88.

Collins, B. and Dunne, T., 1989, Gravel transport, gravel harvesting, and channel-bed degradation in rivers draining the southern Olympic mountains, Washington, U.S.A.: Environmental Geology, v. 13, no. 3, p. 213–224.

Dietrich, W.E., Kirchner, J.W., Ikeda, H., and Iseya, F., 1989, Sediment supply and the development of the coarse surface later in gravel-bedded rivers: Nature, v. 340, no. 6230, p. 215–217.

Edwards, T.K., and Glysson, G.D., 1999, Field methods for measurement of fluvial sediment: U.S. Geological Survey Techniques of Water-Resources Investigations, book 3, chap. C2, 89 p., accessed July 19, 2009, at *http://pubs.usgs.gov/twri/*.

Emmett, W.W., 1980, A field calibration of the sediment-trapping characteristics of the Helley-Smith bedload sampler: U.S. Geological Survey Professional Paper 1139, 44 p.

Gaueman, D.A., Schmidt, J.C., and Wilcock, P.R., 2003, Evaluation of inchannel gravel storage with morphology-based gravel budgets developed from planimetric data: Journal of Geophysical Research, v. 108, no. F1, p. 6001, doi:10.1029/2002JF000002.

Gilbert, G.K., and Murphy, E.C., 1914, The transportation of debris by running water: U.S. Geological Survey Professional Paper 86, p. 263.

Gomez, B., 1991, Bedload transport: Earth-Science Reviews, v. 31, no. 2, p. 89–132.

Gomez, B., and Church, M., 1989, An assessment of bed load sediment transport formulas for gravel bed rivers: Water Resources Research, v. 25, p. 1161–1186.

Gurnell, A.M., 1997, Channel change on the River Dee meanders, 1946–1992, from the analysis of air photographs: Regulated Rivers: Research and Management, v. 13, p. 13–26.

Ham, D.G., and Church, M., 2000, Bed-material transport estimated from channel morphodynamics: Chilliwack River, British Columbia: Earth Surface Processes and Landforms, v. 25, p. 1123–1142.

Harden, D.R., 1995, A comparison of flood-producing storms and their impacts in northwestern California, in Nolan, K.M., Kelsey, H.M., and Marron, D.C., eds., Geomorphic processes and aquatic habitat in the Redwood Creek basin, northwestern California: U.S. Geological Survey Professional Paper 1454, p. D1–D9.

Hickey, J.J., 1969, Variations in low-water streambed elevations at selected stream-gaging stations in northwestern California: U.S. Geological Survey Water-Supply Paper 1879–E, 33 p.

Hicks, D.M., and Gomez, B., 2003, Sediment transport, in Kondolf, G. M. and Piegay, H., eds., Tools in fluvial geomorphology: Chichester, John Wiley and Sons, p. 425–461.

Hoey, T.B., and Ferguson, R., 1994, Numerical simulation of downstream fining by selective transport in gravel-bed rivers: model development and illustration: Water Resources Research, v. 30, p. 2251–2260.

Hughes, M.L., McDowell, P.F., and Marcus, W.A., 2005 [2006], Accuracy assessment of georectified aerial photographs: Implications for measuring lateral channel movement in GIS: Geomorphology, v. 74, p. 1–16.

Jones, J.A., and Grant, G.E., 1996, Long-term stormflow responses to clearcutting and roads in small and large basins, western Cascades, Oregon: Water Resources Research, v. 32, no. 4, p. 959–974.

Jones, J.A., and Grant, G.E., 2001, Comment on "Peak flow responses to clear-cutting and roads in small and large basins, western Cascades, Oregon" by Jones, J.A., and Grant, G.E.: Water Resources Research, v. 37, no. 1, p. 179–180.

Kelsey, H.M., 1980, A sediment budget and an analysis of geomorphic process in the Van Duzen River basin, north coastal California, 1941–1975—Summary: Geological Society of American bulletin, v. 91, no. 4, p. 190–195.

Kelsey, H.M., and Bockheim, J.G., 1994, Coastal landscape evolution as a function of eustasy and surface uplift rate, Cascadia margin, southern Oregon: Geological Society of American Bulletin 106, p. 840–854.

Kelsey, H.M., Coghlan, M., Pitlick, J., and Best, D., 1995, Geomorphic analysis of streamside landslides in the Redwood creek basin, northwestern California, in Nolan, K.M., Kelsey, H.M., and Marron, D.C., eds., Geomorphic processes and aquatic habitat in the Redwood Creek basin, northwestern California: U.S. Geological Survey Professional Paper 1454, p. J1–J12.

Kelsey, H.M., Engebretson, D.C., Mitchell, C.E., and Ticknor, R.L., 1994, Topographic form of the Coast Ranges of the Cascadia margin in relation to coastal uplift rates and plate subduction: Journal of Geophysical Research, v. 99, no. B6 p.12245–12255.

Klingeman, P.C., 1973, Indications of streambed degradation in the Willamette Valley: WRRI–21, Water Resources Research Institute Report WRRI–21, Corvallis, Department of Civil Engineering, Oregon State University, 99 p.

Klingeman, P.C., 1993, Chetco River, Oregon: Hydrologic/hydraulic/morphologic analyses of navigability: Report to Oregon Department of Justice, 47 p.

Kodama, Y., 1994, Downstream changes in the lithology and grain size of fluvial gravels, the Watarase River, Japan; evidence of the role of abrasion in downstream fining: Journal of Sedimentary Research, v. 64, p. 68–75.

Komar, P.D., 1997, The Pacific Northwest coast: Living with the shores of Oregon and Washington: Durham, North Carolina, Duke University Press, 195 p.

Kondolf, G.M., 1994, Geomorphic and environmental effects of instream gravel mining: Landscape and Urban Planning, v. 28, no. 2–3, p. 225–243.

Kondolf, G.M., 1997, Hungry water—Effects of dams and gravel mining on river channels: Environmental Management, v. 21, no. 4, p. 533–551.

Kondolf, G.M., Lisle, T.E., and Wolman, G.M., 2003, Bed sediment measurement, in Kondolf, G.M., and Piegay, H., eds., Tools in fluvial geomorphology: Chichester, John Wiley and Sons, p. 347–395.

Kulm., L.D., and Byrne, J.V., 1966, Sediment response to hydrography in an Oregon estuary: Marine Geology, v. 4, p. 85–118.

Lindsay, J.B., and Ashmore, P.E., 2002, The effects of survey frequency on estimates of scour and fill in a braided river model: Earth Surface Processes and Landforms, v. 27, p. 27–43.

Lisle, T.E., 1981, Recovery of aggraded stream channels at gauging stations in northern California and southern Oregon, Erosion and Sediment Transport in Pacific Rim Steeplands, in Davies, T.R.H., and Pearce, A.J., eds., International Association of Hydrological Sciences: AISH Publication 132, p. 189–211.

Lisle, T.E., 1995, Particle size variations between bed load and bed material in natural gravel bed channels: Water Resources Research, v. 31, no. 4, p. 1107–1118.

Lisle, T.E., Nelson, J.M., Pitlick, J., Madej, M.A., and Barkett, B.L., 2000, Variability of bed mobility in natural, gravel-bed channels and adjustments to sediment load at local and reach scales: Water Resources Research, v. 36, no. 12, p. 3743–3755.

MFG, Inc., Graham Matherws and Associates, and Alice Berg and Associates, 2006, Assessment of the lower Smith River: Report prepared for County of Del Norte, Crescent City, California, 41 p.

Mackin, J.H., 1948, Concept of the graded river: Geological Society of America Bulletin, v. 59, p. 463–512.

Madej, M.A., 1995, Changes in channel-stored sediment, Redwood Creek, northwestern California, 1947 to 1980, in Nolan, K.M., Kelsey, H.M., and Marron, D.C., eds., Geomorphic processes and aquatic habitat in the Redwood Creek basin, northwestern California: U.S. Geological Survey Professional Paper 1454, p. O1–O27.

Maguire, M., 2001, Chetco River watershed assessment: Gold Beach, Oregon, Chetco River Watershed Council by the South Coast Watershed Council, 106 p.

Marquess and Associates, Inc., 1980, Chectco River survey and permit analysis: Medford, Oregon, Marquess and Associates, Inc., 12 p.

Martin, Y., and Church, M., 1995, Bed-material transport estimated from channel surveys–Vedder River, British Columbia: Earth Surface Processes and Landforms, v. 20, p. 347–361.

Martin, Y., and Ham, D., 2005, Testing bedload transport formulae using morphologic transport estimates and field data—lower Fraser River, British Columbia: Earth Surface Processes and Landforms, v. 30, p. 1265–1282.

McLean, D.G., and Church, M., 1999, Sediment transport along lower Fraser River 2—Estimates based on the long-term gravel budget: Water Resources Research, v. 35, no. 8, p. 2549–2559.

Merwade, V.M., Maidment, D.R., and Hodges, B.R., 2005, Geospatial representation of river channels: ASCE Journal of Hydrologic Engineering, v. 10, no. 3, p. 243–251.

Meyer-Peter, E., and Müller, R., 1948, Formulas for bed-transport: Proceedings of the 2nd Congress International Association for Hydraulic Research, Stockholm, Sweden, p. 39–64.

Milhous, R.T., 1973. Sediment transport in a gravel-bottomed stream: Corvallis, Oregon State University, Ph.D. dissertation, 232 p.

Mount, N.J., and Louis, J., 2005, Estimation and propagation of error in the measurement of river channel movement from aerial imagery: Earth Surface Processes and Landforms, v. 30, no. 5, p. 635–643.

Mueller, E.R., Pitlick, J., and Nelson, J.M., 2005, Variation in the reference Shields stress for bed load transport in gravel-bed streams and rivers: Water Resources Research, v. 41, 10 p., W04006, doi: 10.1029/2004WR003692.

O'Connor, J.E., Jones, M.A., and Haluska, T.L., 2003, Flood plain and channel dynamics of the Quinault and Queets Rivers, Washington, USA: Geomorphology, v. 51, p. 31–59.

O'Connor, J.E., Wallick, J.R., Sobieszczyk, S., Cannon, C., and Anderson, S., 2009, Preliminary assessment of vertical stability and grave transport along the Umpqua River, southwestern Oregon: U.S. Geological Survey Open-File Report 2009-1010, 46 p.

Oregon Department of Geology and Mineral Industries, 2009: Lidar collection and mapping—Oregon Lidar Consortium, accessed July 19, 2009, at *http://www.oregongeology.org/sub/projects/olc/default.htm*

Oregon Department of State Lands, 1972, An inventory of filled lands in the Chetco River: Salem, Oregon, Advisory Committee's Engineering Staff for the Advisory Committee to the State Land Board, 15 p.

Orr, E.L., Orr, W.N., and Baldwin, E.M., 1992, Geology of Oregon, 4th ed., Dubuque, Iowa, Kendall/Hunt Publishing, 254 p.

Paola, C., Parker, G., Seal, R., Sinha, S.K., Southard, J.B., and Wilcock, P.R., 1992, Downstream fining by selective deposition in a laboratory flume: Science, v. 258, no. 5089, p. 1757–1760.

Parker, G., 1990a, Surface-based bedload transport relation for gravel rivers: Journal of Hydraulic Research, v. 28, no. 4, p. 417–436.

Parker, G., 1990b, The ACRONYM series of PASCAL programs for computing bedload transport in gravel rivers: St. Anthony Falls Laboratory, University of Minnesota, External Memorandum M–220, 124 p.

Parker, G., and Klingeman, P.C., 1982, On why gravel bed streams are paved: Water Resources Research, v. 18, no. 5, p. 1409–1423.

Parker, G., Klingeman, P.C., and McLean, D.G., 1982, Bedload and size distribution in paved gravel-bed streams: Journal of the Hydraulics Division, Proceedings of the American Society of Civil Engineers, v. 109, no. HY4, p. 54–571.

Peterson, C.D., Scheidegger, P.D., and Komar, P.D., 1982, Sand-dispersal patterns in an active-margin estuary of the northwestern United States as indicated by sand composition, texture and bedforms: Marine Geology, v. 50, p. 77–96.

Pitlick, J., 1992, Flow resistance under conditions of intense gravel transport: Water Resources Research, v. 28, no. 3, p. 891–903.

Pitlick, J., Cui, Y., and Wilcock, P., 2009, Manual for Computing Bed Load Transport Using BAGS (Bedload Assessment for Gravel-bed Streams) Software: Fort Collins, Colorado, U.S. Department of Agriculture, Forest Service, Rocky Mountain Research Station, General Technical Report RMRS–GTR–223, 45 p.

Pitlick, J., Mueller, E.R., Segura, C., Cress, R., and Torizzo, M., 2008, Relation between flow, surface-layer armoring and sediment transport in gravel-bed rivers: Earth Surface Processes and Landforms, v. 33, p. 1192–1209.

Plumley, W.J., 1948, Black Hills terrace gravels–a study in sediment transport: Journal of Geology, v. 56, p. 526–577.

Popov, I.V., 1962, A sediment balance of river reaches and its use for the characteristics of the channel process: Soviet Hydrology, v. 3, p. 249–266.

Raines, M.A., and Kelsey, H.M., 1991, Sediment budget for the Grouse Creek basin, Humboldt County, California: Eureka, California, Six Rivers National Forest, U.S. Department of Agriculture, 110 p., accessed August 1, 2009, at *http://www.waterboards.ca.gov/water_issues/programs/tmdl/records/region_1/2003/ref1719.pdf*

Ramp, L.,1975, Geology and mineral resources of the upper Chetco drainage area, Oregon, including the Kalmiopsis Wilderness and Big Craggies Botanical areas: Oregon Department of Geology and Mineral Industries Bulletin 88, 47 p.

Ratti, F.D., and Kraeg, R.A., 1979, Natural resources of the Chetco River estuary, Final report, Estuary inventory project, Oregon: Oregon Department of Fish and Wildlife for Oregon Land Conservation and Development Commission, v. 2, no. 9, accessed July 24, 2009, at *http://ir.library.oregonstate.edu/jspui/handle/1957/3183*

Reid, L.M., and Dunne, T., 1996, Rapid evaluation of sediment budgets: Reiskirchen, Germany, Catena Verlag GMBH, 164 p.

Reid, L.M., and Dunne, T., 2003, Sediment budgets as an organizing framework in fluvial geomorphology, *in* Kondolf, M., and Piégay, H., eds., Tools in fluvial geomorpholgy: Chichester, John Wiley and Sons, p 463–500.

Rice, K.C., 1999, Trace-element concentrations in streambed sediment across the conterminous United States: Environmental Science and Technology, v. 33, p. 2499–2504.

Ricks, C.L., 1995, Effects of channelization on sediment distribution and aquatic habitat at the mouth of redwood creek, northwestern California, *in* Nolan, K.M., Kelsey, H.M., and Marron, D.C., eds., Geomorphic processes and aquatic habitat in the Redwood Creek basin, northwestern California: U.S. Geological Survey Professional Paper 1454, p. Q1–Q17.

Russell, P.P., 1994, Sediment production and delivery in Pistol River, Oregon and its effects on pool morphology: Corvallis, Oregon State University, MS thesis, 111 p., 29 figs.

Schmidt, J.C., and Wilcock, P.R., 2008, Metrics for assessing the downstream impacts of dams: Water Resources Research, v. 44, 19 p., W04404, doi: 10.1029/2006WR005092

Schumm, S.A., and Stevens, M.A., 1973, Abrasion in place–a mechanism for rounding and size reduction of coarse sediments in rivers: Geology, v. 1, p. 37–40.

Shaw, J., and Kellerhals, R., 1982, The composition of recent alluvial gravels in Alberta river beds: Alberta Research Council Bulletin 41, p. 151.

Slotta, L., and Tang, S., 1976, Chetco River tidal hydrodynamics and associated marina flushing: Final Report: Corvallis, Ocean Engineering Programs, School of Engineering, Oregon State University, Oregon Sea Grant publication, ORESU–T, 76–005, p. 55, accessed July 24, 2009, at *http://nsgl.gso.uri.edu/oresu/oresut76005.pdf.*

Smelser, M.G., and Schmidt, J.C., 1998, An assessment methodology for determining historical changes in mountain streams: U.S. Department of Agriculture, Forest Service, General Technical Report RMRS–GTR–6, 29 p.

Soil Conservation Service, 1979, Flood hazard study, Chetco River, Curry County Oregon: Portland, Oregon, U.S. Department of Agriculture, 29 p.

Stewart, J.H., and LaMarche, V.C., 1967, Erosion and deposition produced by the flood of December 1964, on Coffee Creek, Trinity County, California: U.S. Geological Survey Professional Paper 422–K, 22 p.

Surian, N., and Cisotto, A., 2007, Channel adjustments, bedload transport and sediment sources in a gravel-bed river, Brenta River, Italy: Earth Surface Processes and Landforms, v. 32, p.1641–1656.

U.S. Army Corps of Engineers, 1893, Annual report of the Chief of Engineers, United States Army, to the Secretary of War, for the year 1893 [Part IV]: Washington, U.S. Government Printing Office, 3544 p.

U.S. Army Corps of Engineers, 1939, Chetco River, Oregon—Entrance to Tide Rock—June 20–July 14, 1939 [bathymetric survey]: Portland, Oregon, U.S. Engineer Office, 2 sheets, scale 1:3000.

U.S. Army Corps of Engineers, 2006, HEC–RAS River Analysis System, user's manual, version 4.0 Beta: Davis, California, U.S. Army Corps of Engineers, Institute for Water Resources, Hydrologic Engineering Center, 420 p.

U.S. Environmental Protection Agency, 1999, Van Duzen River and Yaker Creek total maximum daily load for sediment: U.S. Environmental Protection Agency Region IX, 65 p., accessed August 1, 2009 at *http://www.epa.gov/region09/water/tmdl/vanduzen/vanduzen.pdf*

U.S. Forest Service, 2008, Rogue River national forest data library—Geographic information systems: Washington, DC, U.S. Forest Service, accessed February 26, 2009, at *http://www.fs.fed.us/r6/data-library/gis/rogue-river/index.shtml*.

U.S. Forest Service and Bureau of Land Management, 2004, Biscuit fire recovery project, Final environmental impact statement: Medford, Oregon, U.S. Department of Agriculture, Forest Service and U.S. Department of Interior, Bureau of Land Management, [variously paged], accessed July 24, 2009, at *http://www.fs.fed.us/r6/rogue-siskiyou/biscuit-fire/feis.shtml*.

U.S. Geological Survey, 2009, Chetco River sediment transport study: Oregon Water Science Center, U.S. Geological Survey, accessed July 19, 2009, at *http://or.water.usgs.gov/chetco/*.

Waananen, A.O., Harris, P.P., and Williams, R.C., 1971, Floods of December 1964 and January 1965 in the far western state: U.S. Geological Survey Water Supply Paper 1866–A, 265 p.

Wemple, B.C., Jones, J.A., and Grant, G.E., 1996, Channel network extension by logging roads in two basins, western cascades, Oregon: Water Resources Bulletin, v. 32, no. 6, p. 1195–1207.

Wilcock, P.R., 2001, Toward a practical method for estimating sediment-transport rates in gravel-bed rivers: Earth Surface Processes and Landforms, v. 26, no. 13, p. 1395–1408.

Wilcock, P.R., Barta, A.F., Shea, C.C., Kondolf, G.M., Matthes, W.V.G, and Pitlick, J., 1996, Observation of flow and sediment transport entrainment on large gravel-bed river: Water Resources Research, v. 32, p. 2897–2909.

Wilcock, P.R., and Crowe, J.C., 2003, Surface-based transport model for mixed-size sediment: Journal of Hydraulic Engineering, American Society of Civil Engineers, v. 129, p. 120–128.

Wilcock, P., Pitlick, J., and Cui, Y., 2009, Sediment transport primer—Estimating bed-material transport in gravel-bed rivers: Fort Collins, Colorado, U.S. Department of Agriculture, Forest Service, Rocky Mountain Research Station, General Technical Report RMRS–GTR–226, 78 p.

Wolman, M.G., 1954, A method for sampling coarse river-bed material: American Geophysical Union Transactions: v. 35, p. 951-956.